W9-BVB-695

the quality of their personal and professional lives. This is a guidebook for anyone seeking personal transformation and a more purposeful life."
—Jay Samit, adjunct professor, USC Viterbi School of Engineering, bestselling author of *Disrupt You!*

"Sam has a special talent at helping you recognize and then achieve what you really want. She's one of the reasons my first book exists. I highly recommend her book to anyone who's stuck or wants to turn their dreams into reality."
—Kamal Ravikant, bestselling author of *Love Yourself Like Your Life Depends On It*, *Live Your Truth*, and *Rebirth*

"Are you happy with your life and work as they are—or are you ready to reinvent yourself and reimagine your future? Sam Horn's essential new book will inspire you and show you the path to create a meaningful, rewarding next act—starting today."
—Dorie Clark, author of *Reinventing You* and adjunct professor, Duke University Fuqua School of Business

SOMEDAY IS NOT A DAY IN THE WEEK

Also by Sam Horn

IDEApreneur: Monetize Your Mind

Got Your Attention?:
How to Create Intrigue and Connect with Anyone
Current Quotes: Intriguing Insights from Today's Top Icons, Influencers and
Innovators

Pop!: Create the Perfect Pitch, Title, and Tagline for Anything

Tongue Fu!® at School: 30 Ways to Get Along With Teachers, Principals,
Students, and Parents

Take the Bully by the Horns: Stop Unethical, Uncooperative, or Unpleasant
People from Ruining Your Life

ConZentrate: Get Focused and Pay Attention—When Life Is Filled with
Pressures, Distractions, and Multiple Priorities

What's Holding You Back?: 30 Days to Having the Courage and Confidence
to Do What You Want, Meet Whom You Want, and Go Where You Want

Create Confidence: A 30-Day Program for
an Unshakable Foundation of Self-Assurance

Tongue Fu!®: How to Deflect, Disarm, and Defuse Any Verbal Conflict

Crisp: Concentration!: How to Focus for Success (Fifty Minute Series)

SOMEDAY
Is Not a Day in the Week

10 Hacks to Make the Rest of Your
Life the Best of Your Life

SAM HORN

St. Martin's Press ❦ New York

www.stmartins.com

Designed by Patrice Sheridan

LIBRARY OF CONGRESS CATALOGING-IN-PUBLICATION DATA

Names: Horn, Sam, author.
Title: Someday is not a day in the week : 10 hacks to make the rest of your life
    the best of your life / Sam Horn.
Description: First [edition]. | New York : St. Martin's Press, 2019.
Identifiers: LCCN 2018045707 | ISBN 9781250201225 (hardcover) |
    ISBN 9781250201232 (ebook)
Subjects: LCSH: Success. | Time management.
Classification: LCC BJ1611.2 .H67 2019 | DDC 158—dc23
LC record available at https://lccn.loc.gov/2018045707

Our books may be purchased in bulk for promotional, educational, or business use.
Please contact your local bookseller or the Macmillan Corporate and
Premium Sales Department at 1-800-221-7945, extension 5442,
or by email at MacmillanSpecialMarkets@macmillan.com.

First Edition: March 2019

10   9   8   7   6   5   4   3   2   1

I have always imagined that Paradise will be a kind of library.

—Jorge Luis Borges

This book is dedicated to librarians everywhere for

the pivotal role you play in giving us dreams, ideas,

and stories that remind us there's a big world out there

waiting for us to discover it.

Contents

SOMEDAY IS NOT A DAY IN THE WEEK

Introduction

"The thing is, we think we have time."

—BUDDHA

My dad thought he had time. His dream was to visit all the National Parks when he retired. As Director of Vocational Ag Education for the state of California, he spent five or six days a week driving hundreds of miles to high schools and county fairs to advise FFA (Future Farmers of America) students on their projects. He was an honorable man who felt a deep obligation to make an enduring difference for the people in his programs. He achieved that goal. But at a cost.

Dad finally took off on his long-delayed dream a week after he retired. A week after that, he had a stroke in a hotel bathroom. Dad never got to visit the Grand Tetons, the Great Smoky Mountains, Banff, or Zion. He never got to do what he had dreamed of doing his whole life.

I don't want that to happen to me.

I don't want that to happen to you.

I don't want that to happen to anyone.

The good news is, you don't need to quit your job, win the lottery, or walk away from your responsibilities to make your life more of what you want it to be.

There are things you can do *right here, right now* to be happier, healthier, and more fulfilled.

I'm speaking from experience.

Three years ago, I took my business on the road for a Year by the Water.

It was a marvelous experience, but it wasn't the *places* I visited that stood out, it was the *people* I met. In particular, the people who told me, "*Someday* I'm going to do something like that."

The thing is, as my dad and millions like him have discovered the hard way, *someday* is not a day in the week.

As Paulo Coelho says, "One day you will wake up and there won't be any more time to do the things you've always wanted. One Day or Day One. You decide."

I hope this book is Day One of the rest of your life.

I hope the adventures and insights you're about to read inspire you to realize that today is the only day you have for sure and you choose to live accordingly.

I hope you choose to stop waiting and start creating the quality of life you want, need, and deserve now—not later.

Why Every Chapter Starts with a Story

"The world is not made up of atoms; it's made up of stories."

—Muriel Rukeyser

If you enjoy reading inspirational books like *Wild* or *Eat, Pray, Love*, you're in the right place. It's reassuring to read someone's story and realize, "You mean I'm not the only one who has struggled or who has felt like that?" It is motivating to see how other people have been able to get clear on what they want, overcome challenges, and change their life—for good.

That's why every chapter in this book starts with a story, a story from me or from people I've met along the way. People who live in small towns and big cities. People of all ages and all ethnic and economic backgrounds. People who realized the clock was ticking and decided to do something differently instead of wait for the proverbial someday that will never come.

An engineer named Bob said, "Stories are nice but I'm a left-brainer. I like spreadsheets and blueprints. Do you provide a process we can follow to make this easy to understand and apply?"

Good question, Bob. After reviewing my lessons learned and those of the people I've interviewed, I realized there are *steps* many of us have taken to make our life more fulfilling.

I call these steps *Life Hacks*, based on a colleague who modeled how hacking can tap into proven best practices, expedite results, and offer a shortcut to success.

Dave Asprey was a three-hundred-pound computer whiz. He was a genius at his job but was a frustrated single guy. No matter what diet he tried or how hard he exercised, he couldn't lose weight.

One day, he had an epiphany. "If I can hack computers, I bet I can hack my own biology."

You may know the rest of that story. Based on his research, Dave discovered the health-improving powers of pure coconut oil. He created BulletProof Coffee, which has grown into a global empire with a podcast and an annual summit. Dave is walking, talking proof of what can happen when you hack what isn't working and create something that does. He is a vibrant entrepreneur, father, and husband who loves his life, family, business, and good health.

I thought, "If Dave can do it, so can I." And so can you.

The Ten Life Hacks for Turning Someday into Today

*"A real decision is measured by the fact that you've taken a new action.
If there's no action, you haven't truly decided."*

—TONY ROBBINS

The Ten Life Hacks, reflected in this book's ten sections, are *actions* you can take to create a more fulfilling life, sooner, not later. Please note: These hacks are a *framework*, not a *formula*.

I'm not saying that if you do all of them, happiness is guaranteed. That would be hubris.

I am saying, "These are happiness dots I've collected, connected, and curated that have helped me and others improve our quality of life. I'm sharing them in the hopes they might be of interest and value to you. Please take what resonates *with* you and works *for* you."

Remember those coloring books we had growing up where you drew between the numbered dots to see what emerged? The picture became clear—"Aha. It's a cat!"—as you connected the dots.

That's what I hope happens with these Life Hacks. As you read these chapters and act on the Hacks, the dots will connect as to how to create a more authentic life. A clearer picture will emerge of what you want your life to look and feel like. It will, all of a sudden, make more sense.

LIFE HACK 1:   **Evaluate** Your Happiness History

LIFE HACK 2:   **Generate** a Today, Not Someday Dream

LIFE HACK 3:   **Abdicate** Outdated Beliefs and Behaviors

LIFE HACK 4:   **Initiate** Daily Actions that Move Your Life Forward

LIFE HACK 5:   **Celebrate** What's Right with Life, Right Here, Right Now

LIFE HACK 6:   **Affiliate** with People Who Have Your Back and Front

LIFE HACK 7:   **Integrate** Your Passion and Profession

LIFE HACK 8:   **Negotiate** for What You Want, Need, and Deserve

LIFE HACK 9:   **Innovate** a Fresh Start

LIFE HACK 10:   **Relocate** to Greener Pastures

How to Get the Most Value from This Book

"Has first baseman Don Mattingly exceeded expectations?"

—A REPORTER

"I'd say he's done more than that."

—YOGI BERRA

If you want this book to exceed your expectations, keep a pen in hand so you can make notes in the margins and answer the questions in the Readers' Guide at the back of the book. The more actively you involve yourself in reading this book, the more likely you are to turn your intentions into life-changing results.

In fact, as suggested in chapter 13, you'll get even more value from this book if you purchase a Someday Journal (or the equivalent) and take five minutes every morning to write how you'll use these Life Hacks to make that day more rewarding.

One more suggestion? You might want to read this book in tandem with a friend or host your own Someday Salon or book club. (Instructions on how to do that on the SOMEDAY is Not a Day in the Week website.)

What's a Someday Salon? It's an interactive evening where people fill out the Four-Minute–Four-Box Happiness Quiz (see page 13), discuss their answers, and identify a meaningful NEXT. The goal is to create a community where everyone has opportunities to connect and contribute stories about what's working in their life, what's not, and what they're going to do about it.

You don't have to be a trained facilitator to do this (although that is an option). Hosting a salon is a fun way to practice all the Life Hacks—e.g., generating, affiliating, celebrating—at once.

Just know in advance that *people will appreciate this opportunity to discuss what really matters and won't want to leave.* At our first salon in Denver, Colorado, parents were calling their babysitters and begging for an extra hour or two so they could stay and continue their conversations.

As John, a self-described techie, told me, "I don't go to networking events anymore because I dread small talk. This was the opposite of that. I had more interesting, genuine conversations in the last two hours than I have had in ten years of attending mixers."

Temple Grandin says, "People are always looking for the single magic bullet that will totally change everything. There is no single magic bullet."

Temple's right. There are no magic bullets. There are breadcrumbs, though, that have the power to educate us, inspire us, and sustain us.

The adventures and insights in the book are breadcrumbs that can help you leverage people's hard-won wisdom so you don't have to figure everything out on your own.

I hope you'll follow this trail of breadcrumbs and integrate these Life Hacks into your life. I promise, you will never regret clarifying what's truly important and bringing more of that into your life; you'll only regret not doing it *sooner*. Onward.

EVALUATE
Your Happiness History

"In the name of God, stop a moment, cease your
work, look around you."

—Leo Tolstoy

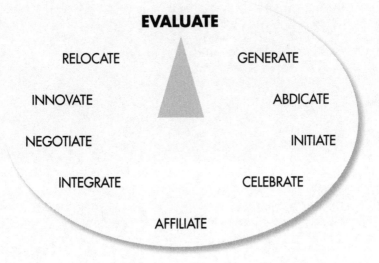

EVALUATE

RELOCATE		GENERATE
INNOVATE		ABDICATE
NEGOTIATE		INITIATE
INTEGRATE		CELEBRATE
	AFFILIATE	

The first Life Hack is to stop, look around, reflect, and EVALUATE what's been contributing to your quality of life; what's been compromising it. The Four-Minute–Four-Box Happiness Quiz can offer surprising insights into what's supporting your life satisfaction, and what's not.

1

Play Hooky for a Day

"Exhaustion is not a status symbol."

— BRENÉ BROWN

had just wrapped up an intense two-day consulting job in Southern California. I was sitting in my rental car, trying to drum up the energy to drive to the airport and catch a plane back to D.C.

My phone rang. It was my son, Andrew, who was helping me with my business. He must have sensed something in my voice because he asked, "Whazzup, Mom?"

"Andrew, I'm so exhausted, I don't even know how I'm going to get on the plane tonight. I've got to take a red-eye and then turn around in a couple days and fly back to the West Coast."

He paused, then decided to jump in. "Mom, there's something about you I don't understand. You've created a life where you can do anything you want and you're not taking advantage of it."

Wow. Out of the mouths of twenty-somethings.

He didn't stop there, "Why don't you stay there the next few days? I'll book you a hotel and you can handle your business from there."

Andrew was right. No one was forcing me to fly back to the East

Coast. I was my own boss. I *could* do what I wanted. A half hour later, I was checking into the Laguna Beach Hotel. A half hour later, I was falling asleep to the sounds of the ocean outside my open window. Bliss.

The next day I followed another piece of Andrew's advice. He had said, "Mom, you've been working so hard, you deserve a break. Why don't you play hooky for a day? I've got this."

What a concept. As a single mom and small business owner, I'd been going nonstop for decades. The thought of waking up when I wanted and not having back-to-back appointments all day made me feel like a little kid getting away with something.

Sleeping in the next morning was sumptuous. I dawdled over a cup of coffee and then headed into town to explore. As I strolled Main Street, I was drawn as if by a magnet to a bookstore. I gravitated to the writers' section and started thumbing through old favorites by Anne Lamott and Julia Cameron. As I did a voice welled up in me, "*I am a writer. That's who I am.*"

The voice was as real as if someone were speaking to me. Actually, someone *was* speaking to me. The author I'd buried in busyness. The author who spent most of her time consulting, who'd had no time to work on a new book for two years.

Please understand, I was grateful for my career. Katharine Graham of *The Washington Post* said, "To do what you love and feel that it matters, how could anything be more fun?" Well, the only thing that could be more fun is to do work you love with people you enjoy and respect *and get paid for it.* That's what I got to do, so I was not looking a gift source (intentional) in the mouth.

Still, what this day of hooky was bringing up was that I had set aside a passion for my profession. I spent most of my time helping other people get their work out in the world instead of getting my own work out in the world. And it was taking a toll on my soul.

Standing in that bookstore, inspired by the muse, I promised myself I'd get up early every morning and write, just like bestselling author John Grisham did before he hit it big with his blockbusters. I headed back to my hotel, turned the desk so it faced the ocean, and spent the rest of that day gazing out at the water and drafting my next book.

Gloria Steinem said, "Writing is the only thing that when I do it, I don't feel I should be doing something else." That's how writing feels to me too. When I'm getting thoughts out of my head and onto paper (or my laptop), I feel like I'm doing what I was born to do. The world slips away and I am in my element. What does that for you?

What Would You Do If You Could Play Hooky?

"Tomorrow is another day. But so was yesterday."
—RENE RICARD

What is it that, when you're doing it, you don't want to be doing anything else? How long has it been since you've had time to do that?

If you could play hooky for a day—and there would be no repercussions and your responsibilities would be taken care of—what would you do?

A thirty-something named Carl said, "If I could play hooky for a day, I'd spend it in a garden digging my hands into the soil and planting things. I grew up on a farm. My parents put me in charge of our family garden when I was ten. I felt so grown up that they entrusted me with that. I spent hours watering, weeding, planting, and picking. I loved it so much I wasn't even aware of the passage of time. I left home for college and then stayed here in the city to work. I didn't realize until right now how much gardening meant to me and how much I miss it."

I told him, "When you have something that makes you feel that good, it's like having the answers to the test. There's no mystery about what would make you happier. All you need to do is find a garden and start spending some time in it."

He said, "Sam, I live in an apartment building downtown. That's not going to happen."

"Get creative. I bet there's a community garden somewhere near you. Or maybe even a botanical garden that welcomes volunteers. Could you check that out?"

Guess what? Carl now spends a couple mornings a month in the potting shed and greenhouse of a friend who's a commercial landscaper. He told me, "This is ideal. I get to dig my hands in the dirt and work with plants whenever I want—or not—and it doesn't cost a thing."

When You Daydream . . .
What Do You Daydream About?

"If you ask people, 'What is your passion,' they often freeze.
They feel as if they have to give an amazing answer like
'Feed the world's orphans.'"

—DAN PINK

Please understand, what you do on your day of hooky doesn't have to be grandiose. Like Dan Pink said, it doesn't have to be "amazing" or noble. This is *your* day. You get to do exactly what you want without apologies or "shoulds." It can be a bucket list of things you've been putting off or an all-day nap. You have complete freedom to do what's been calling you.

Still not sure what that might be? This Happiness Quiz can help. It only takes a few minutes and can help you identify specific things that could make you happier *now*, not someday.

Here's how to take the quiz. Have you ever played a word-association game in which someone asks a question, and you're supposed to say the first thing that comes to mind? That's what you want to do here. Please write down whatever pops into your mind, even if it's not "nice." No one needs to see this unless you want them to. You won't be graded on your answers; it's not like a job interview where you're supposed to say something like "I'm a perfectionist. I don't stop until I get it right" when you're asked "What's your weakness?" If you tell the truth, and nothing but the truth, this little quiz can clarify what's not working in your life and what you'd rather do so you can start making positive changes.

The Four-Minute–Four-Box Happiness Quiz

Square 1. "What are you *doing* in your life that you *want to do?*" Walking your dog? Reading? Running your own business? Having date nights with your spouse?

Square 2. "What are you *not doing* in your life that you *want to do?*" Not losing weight? Not changing jobs? Not exercising? Not spending time with friends? Not having sex?

Square 3. "What are you *doing* in your life that you *don't want to do?*" Commuting? Racking up credit-card debt? Fighting with a family member? Watching too much TV?

Square 4. "What are you *not doing* in your life that you *don't want to do?*" Yes, this is a double negative. It's an important question though because it identifies unhealthy behaviors you're keeping out of your life. Maybe you used to smoke, don't anymore, and you're happy about that.

	Doing	Not Doing
Want to	1	2
Don't Want to do	3	4

Analyzing the Results from the Happiness Quiz

*"They always say time changes things, but you actually
have to change them yourself."*

—ANDY WARHOL

When you're finished, look at the responses in Squares 1 and 4. That's what's *right* with your life. This is what is contributing to your happiness.

Now, look at the answers in Squares 2 and 3. That's what's *wrong* with your life. This is what is compromising your happiness.

Please note, none of us is perfect so we'll always have responses in Squares 2 and 3. You know what the question is? *How long? How long* have you been doing these things you *don't* want to do? *How long* have you *not* been doing things you want to do?

John Foster Dulles said, "The mark of a successful organization isn't whether it has problems; it's whether it has the same problems it had last year." The same is true of us. As humans, we'll always have problems. The question is, are they the *same* problems we had last year and the year before that? If so, that's a good indicator we're living in *someday* land.

"*Somedays*" lurk in Squares 2 and 3. These are priorities we've been telling ourselves we'll act on *someday* when we have more time, money, whatever. These are regrets waiting to happen.

Maybe you're thinking, "Sam, give me a break. I'm working sixty hours a week. I don't have the luxury to act on the things in Squares 2 and 3."

I understand. The good news is, you don't need to change everything at once. That's not realistic. If you take action on *one thing* in Square 2 or 3, it can set up a positive ripple effect that compensates for other aspects of your life that are not to your liking. What's *your* one thing?

Doing One Thing Differently Can Set up a Positive Ripple Effect

"Is there ever any particular spot where one can put one's finger and say, 'It all began that day, at such a time and such a place, with such an incident?'"

— AGATHA CHRISTIE

Guess what the most frequent answer in Square 3 is? *Social media.* Specifically, spending too much time online mindlessly scrolling Facebook, Instagram, Twitter, and other online forums.

One woman told me, "I read an article about tech addiction. I'm embarrassed to admit this but I have all the signs. It is pretty much what I do anytime I have spare time."

I asked, "Have you seen the research that says the more time we spend online, the more lonely, depressed, and unhappy we are? I think social media is the catch-22 of happiness. Not only does the constant comparison to other people's lives sabotage our self-esteem, it gobbles up hours we could be using for more meaningful activities. How do you plan to change this?"

"That article suggested we have rules. No phone in the bedroom or during meals. Schedule two social media times a day and never as soon as we wake up or just before we go to bed. I'm going to hold myself accountable for changing this, because I already know that when I look back at my life, I will regret wasting so much time on something that won't matter in the long run."

I told her, "That is a perfect example of how *one thing* can positively impact *everything.* It can improve your relationship with your kids, your husband, and your friends because you're giving them your full attention instead of distractedly checking your phone. It can free up time to journal or read a good book or get outside for a walk instead of spending hours staring at a little piece of plastic. It can reverse a mindless habit that adds no enduring value and can open up time for more uplifting activities. Good for you for setting up that positive ripple effect."

Find a Better Way

"There's a way to do it better—find it."

—THOMAS EDISON

Want another example of someone who changed one thing that set up a positive ripple effect?

A man in one of my workshops said, "I grew up playing just about every sport our school offered. Being an athlete was my identity. I married my college sweetheart and we had three kids. She died in an automobile accident when our sons were twelve, fourteen, and sixteen. I moved back to Minnesota so my mom and dad could help raise the boys. I've been working two jobs since then to make ends meet and save enough money to put them through college.

"All my answers in Squares 2 and 3 were around my health and weight. What I was *doing* that I *didn't want* to do was eating everything in sight and being a couch potato. What I *wasn't doing* that I *wanted* to do was working out, playing sports, and meeting women.

"Filling out that quiz helped me realize it was past time for me to do something about this. I went online and discovered our local shopping mall has a walking club that meets three mornings a week. That was perfect for me because it's free; it's inside (we have long, cold winters); it's at 7:30 a.m. so I can get in my walk and still get to work on time. Plus, it's a way to get back into shape without killing myself. The best part? I'm *meeting women!* We circuit the mall six times and talk the whole way. It's the best thing I've done for myself in years."

I love his story because it shows, once again, how doing *one thing* differently can improve our happiness on multiple levels.

Baseball player Mickey Mantle said, "If I knew I was going to live this long, I would have taken better care of myself." Are you taking care of yourself? Now that you've identified a priority in Square 2 or 3 where you are *not* taking care of something important to you, the next step is to envision how you intend to do it differently.

What *Won't* You Do on Your Day of Hooky?

"Life moves pretty fast. If you don't stop and look around once in a while, you could miss it."

— FERRIS BUELLER

Did you see John Hughes's movie *Ferris Bueller's Day Off*? In it, lead character Matthew Broderick skips school with some friends. He "borrows" a Ferrari and they cruise around Chicago, catching a Cubs game, dining at a four-fork restaurant, and joining a parade. Their goal is to "carpe diem"—to seize the day and *have the time of their life*.

Look at that phrase, *have the time of their life*. Are you *having* the time of your life or are you *wasting* the time of your life? Are you *seizing* the day or waiting for *some* day?

There is another insight from that movie worth noting. When Ferris's friends ask, "What are we going to do with our day of hooky?" he smiles and says, "The question isn't what *are* we going to do. The question is, what *aren't* we going to do?"

When considering how to spend your day of hooky, it may be easier to start with what you *aren't* going to do. Ferris didn't want to waste a beautiful spring day sitting inside at a desk. He wanted to have fun with his friends while they still could, before they all went their separate ways.

How about you? What are you *not* going to do on *your* day? Remember, this is a pretend day so you don't have to be practical. You get to do exactly as you please, so use your imagination.

Are you thinking, "I've got so much going on, there's no way I can take a day off."

That's what Jenelle, a twenty-something told me. She said, "I'm taking a full load of courses and waitressing to pay my way through college. If I'm not in class, I'm studying or at the restaurant. I don't have a free afternoon, much less a free day."

Understood. If that's the case with you, play hooky in your mind and imagine *a hooky hour*. What would give you a well-deserved break from your have-tos?

As you'll discover in chapter 10, it's not selfish to carve out an hour to do something you enjoy; it can compensate for parts of your life you can't control.

Now that you've explored what could put the light in your eyes, it's time to identify what other factors have influenced your happiness—for better or for worse.

2

Remember the Golden Days

"Success is not about wealth, fame or power,
but how many shining eyes I have around me."

—BEN ZANDER

was surrounded by shining eyes. It was my birthday, a significant one, and friends and family had flown in from around the country to join me for a weekend celebration. We started with a "This Is Your Life" quiz show with friends Mary and Denise asking questions of the crowd to see if they knew: "Which is of these is true? That Sam played tennis at the White House and President Ford's Golden Retriever stole the tennis balls? That Sam gave gum to her 4-H sheep to keep them quiet during county fair judging contests? Or that Sam competed in the Folsom Rodeo barrel-racing competition when she was in college?" Answer? All of them.

The next day we went for a walk around the lake and returned for a home-cooked meal, whipped up from scratch by epicurean Judy Gray. We sat around "talking-story," as they say in Hawaii. Nisha shared highlights of her recent trip to Egypt including her visit with a shaman. A left-brainer who's not a fan of spirituality said, "I don't know what to do with shamans." Judy piped up from the kitchen, "Just don't squeeze them." (You may need to be a boomer to remember this tagline from the famous Charmin commercial with Mr. Whipple.)

Someone mentioned they'd heard great things about the movie *Midnight in Paris* so we spontaneously decided to go. In that movie, the lead character, a novelist played by Owen Wilson, longs to go back to the era when Ernest Hemingway, F. Scott Fitzgerald, Salvador Dalí, and Gertrude Stein hung out together in Paris. Through filmmaking magic (and suspension of disbelief), Owen's character gets his wish and is whooshed back to the jazzy café society of the 1920s, where he gets to kibitz with these creative geniuses.

Toward the end of the movie, a woman finds out Owen Wilson's character, Gil, has time-traveled and begs him to share the magic formula so she can go back to the seventeenth century and meet Rembrandt.

Gil takes her by the shoulders and beseeches her to understand what he's discovered, that happiness is not being in another time or place with the rich and famous, it is being right here, right now, with people you love.

He implores her, "No, *these* are the golden days, *these* are the golden times." She doesn't listen to him. She's convinced that happiness exists somewhere, sometime, else.

I knew it then and I know it now.

Anytime we are fortunate to be with people we love, *those* are the golden times. Every day we wake up and are blessed with health, *those* are the golden days. Every moment that we have the freedom of movement to be outside and experience Mother Nature's marvels, *those* are the golden moments. Every hour we get to do something we're good at that matters, *those* are the golden hours.

How about you? When have you experienced a golden day? When was there a time when all was right with your world and you were deeply happy?

In this chapter, we'll explore what it will take for you to have more golden days. One way to do that is to get clear on your True Priorities and your Time Priorities to see if they match. If they do, you're living a life in alignment with your values. If they don't, we've got work to do.

Are You Living an Aligned Life?

"Remember how far you've come, not how far you have to go."

—RICK WARREN

Starting from the top, what are the five things most important to you? What do you value most? Family? Friends? Health? Career? Faith? Giving back? Pets? Politics? Hobbies? Legacy?

TRUE PRIORITIES

    1. _____

    2. _____

    3. _____

    4. _____

    5. _____

Now, in descending order, what do you spend the most time on every week?

TIME PRIORITIES

    1. _____

    2. _____

    3. _____

    4. _____

    5. _____

Now, compare the two lists. Does the second list look anything like the first list?

This can be quite an eye-opener. A forty-something participant named Bryan said, "Sam, if I had to leave the workshop right now, that priority exercise would have made the whole thing worthwhile. I put Family first. Health second. Faith third. Giving back fourth. And Learning fifth because I'm always trying to grow.

"Guess how I spend most of my time? If I'm honest about it, and I want to be, work is numbers 1, 2, and 3. Family squeezes in number 4. Faith is a distant number 5, as I only go to church once or twice a month. I am not spending any time on my health or hobbies. I used to play guitar but haven't picked one up in years. I don't have time to take classes, or go to conferences, so I'm not learning anything. What a wake-up call. I'm not sure what I can do about this though."

I told him, "The first step is to pick an overlooked item from your first list—which is your True Priorities list—and make time for it this week."

One of my favorite stories that demonstrates how acting on one True Priority can make a *big* difference, came from an orthodontist. He told me, "What was number one on my Time Priorities list? Work. I spend fifty to sixty hours a week at my office putting braces on teeth. No one is happy to see me. Parents are concerned about how much it's going to cost. Kids worry about how long it's going to take and if it's going to hurt. The thing is, by most people's standards, I'm successful. I have my own business, I have ten people working for me and I make good money. But this isn't what I want to be doing."

I asked, "What do you want to be doing?"

"You know what I had on my True Priorities list? Astronomy. That's what lit me up in high school. I grew up reading sci-fi. I got a telescope for my tenth birthday and spent many nights gazing up at the galaxies. But when it was time to pick a college major, my parents told me I needed to get serious about a sensible career because no one was going to pay me to look at the stars. So, I applied to dental school and here I am."

Fast-forward to a happy ending. We brainstormed how he could compensate for what he didn't like with something he did. He didn't want to abandon his practice, he just wanted something to be happy about. He now drives to UC Berkeley's observatory every week to study with a world-renowned astronomer. He said with a smile, "I guess you can say I have stars in my eyes again."

How about you? What did you learn from those two lists? Is what you say is important what you actually spend your time on? Are your Time Priorities aligned with your True Priorities? The more they are, the more "golden days" you'll have. If not, what is one thing you will do this week to give a neglected priority the time and attention it deserves?

Conduct a Happiness Interview

"It's the people who don't ask questions who remain clueless."

— NEIL deGRASSE TYSON

Now that you've compared your True Priorities with your Time Priorities, it's time to get a clue about what else has shaped your happiness up until now. These ten questions can help do that. To get the most value from your interview, you might want to follow these guidelines.

+ Just as you did with the Happiness Quiz, express how you really feel. It doesn't do anyone any good to give "politically correct" answers that tiptoe around buried issues.

+ Go online and get the rev.com app so you can record your answers. A friend tells me that if she's ever feeling worn down, she listens again to her interview. It re-centers her and re-inspires her to do one thing every day to make it a good day, maybe even a golden day.

+ Take this book and a trusted friend to lunch. Having someone interview you allows the luxury of immersing yourself in an uninterrupted stream-of-consciousness state of flow. Some of us are reluctant to go deep because we're not sure people want to hear it. This is your chance to get it all out to a supportive listener. (It can be their turn next time.)

+ Get out your calendar, call your friend, and schedule your Happiness Interview right now. This is a gift you're giving yourself.

Please note: Your interviewer doesn't have to be in the same city. You can do this by Skype or FaceTime. I know two sisters from the East and West Coast who interviewed each other by phone. They both said it was one of the most meaningful conversations they've had in years. "No one knows me better than my sister. We have fifty years of shared history together so swapping stories and going down Memory Row was a joy." Okay, ready to begin? Start your voice recorder. Ready, set, respond.

1. On a scale of 1 to 10, how happy are you currently? Who and what is contributing to your happiness? Who and what is causing you to be unhappy? Explain.

2. What was your family like growing up? Were you a happy kid? Why or why not? How about your siblings? Parents? Was it a happy home—or not so much? How does that continue to impact you?

3. Fill in this sentence, "If it weren't too late, I'd _____." (What? Travel more? Start my own business? Search for my soul mate?) Why do you believe it's too late? Is that true?

4. Who is someone you know who is happy? Why do you think they are? Be specific.

5. "If I were to right-size my life and stuff, I would let go of _____."

6. What's preventing you from releasing, quitting, getting rid of, cleaning, or clearing that up?

7. Finish this sentence, "Money is _____." How would you describe your financial situation now? Do you have enough money? How much do you need/want? Do you trust you'll have enough for retirement? Why or why not?

8. Let's talk about your body. Are you fit, vital, physically active, sick, in pain? On a scale of 1 to 10, how would you rate your health now? How is that impacting your quality of life?

9. On a scale of 1 to 10, how fulfilled are you by your work? What *do* you like about it? What *don't* you like about it? Are you in the right job, right career? Explain your answer.

10. Think about the people in your personal and professional life:
    a. Professional life: Do you like, enjoy, and respect who you work with, for, and around? If so, how so? If not, why not and how does that impact you on a daily basis?
    b. Personal life: Do your significant others (family members, spouse, friends, neighbors) support your happiness? If so, how so? If not, what's a specific example?
11. Have you ever had a calling? Something you felt you were born to do? Did you pursue that dream or passion project? If so, how did that turn out for you? If it didn't work out, why not?

What to Do *After* Your Happiness Interview

"The life you've led doesn't need to be the only life you have."
— ANNA QUINDLEN

Many people tell me this Happiness Interview was an unexpectedly profound experience.

For example, one woman said, "It wasn't until I did that Happiness Interview that I realized how much my parents modeled unhappiness and how much it still affects my brother and me. They were borderline hoarders and obsessive compulsives. Our house was such a mess; it was embarrassing and depressing. My brother and I never had friends over. I can't remember ever having a family dinner conversation where we talked about our day, enjoyed each other's company, or where my parents encouraged us. My brother and I couldn't wait to get away."

I asked her, "How does your upbringing affect your happiness now?"

She said, on the brink of tears, "I always thought happiness wasn't in the cards for me. Then you said we can use our past as an *excuse* or as *incentive*; that our happiness as adults should depend on what we're doing *now*, not on what happened decades ago. You shared Abraham Lincoln's quote, 'Most people are about as happy as they make up their minds to be.' That struck a chord with me. I am making up my mind to be happy instead of continuing to blame my parents for why I'm un-happy."

How about you? Did you have an epiphany as a result of the Happiness Interview? What is one thing you can and will do to start liking yourself and your life a little bit more, starting today?

And if you're waiting until you have more time to take action, keep reading. You're about to discover that happiness doesn't require *more* time, it requires that you stop waiting for the *right* time. The next few chapters show how.

3

Adopt a Sense of Urgency

> "My mother always told me I wouldn't amount to anything because I procrastinate. I said, 'Just wait.'"
>
> —JUDY TENUTA

Okay, back to that day of hooky in Laguna Beach when I promised to pull a John Grisham and write first thing every morning. That's not what happened. My good intentions lasted a couple weeks, then I got busy and missed a few mornings. The next thing I knew my writing project was on the shelf again.

It took a health scare to shake me out of my rut and motivate me to stop procrastinating.

I'd been battling a respiratory infection for weeks, but "soldiered" through it because I had places to be, people counting on me. I kept hoping it would get better. It didn't.

One morning I was so sick I couldn't get out of bed. A friend rushed me to Urgent Care. After checking my lungs and reviewing my X-rays, the doctor diagnosed walking pneumonia. While writing out the prescription, he asked, "Why did you wait so long to get this taken care of?"

I made some mealy-mouthed excuse about being too busy to go to the doctor. He shrugged and said, "You're lucky. I'm giving you a Z-Pack and you'll be better in ten days. But this was a warning. If you don't start taking better care of yourself, your body will do something more drastic to get your attention."

Well that got my attention. But it wasn't until a few weeks later when a dream "downloaded" (more about that in the next chapter) that I finally had sufficient incentive to stop putting off what I really wanted to do and turn my "Someday I wish" into a "Today I will."

What Are You Postponing?

"Life, as it is called, is for most of us one long postponement."

— Henry Miller

The question is, why did I postpone what was calling me? Why do so many of us procrastinate on our True Priorities when we know they would make us happier and healthier? We're supposed to know better, right? Yet many of us continue to put off what's important to us, optimistically assuming we'll have the option to do them later.

A young father named Jeff told me, "I don't dream anymore. It's too painful. I just keep my head down, put one foot in front of the other, and do the best I can."

Ouch. When I asked what he meant, he said, "I love my wife and kids. I really do. But my life is nothing like I thought it would be. My wife and I both work full time. One of our sons has special needs. He never sleeps through the night so we go nonstop all day, every day. Maybe someday I'll have the luxury to dream but I don't see that happening any time soon."

Jeff's story was a variation of what many people told me, "Doing what I want is just not an option. I've got too many obligations to think about that now."

Which brings us to the *core* of this book. Many people feel *their life is not their own.* And they feel powerless to change it. "It's just the way it is," they tell me.

No. It's not "just the way it is." Certainly, there are some things beyond our control. Having a child with special needs is beyond our control. Having a parent with dementia is beyond our control. Our company going bankrupt and putting us out of work is beyond our control.

Yet, as Victor Frankl pointed out in his classic *Man's Search for Meaning*, "Everything can be taken from a man but one thing—the last of the human freedoms, to choose one's attitude in any given set of circumstances, to choose one's own way." In other words, we may not be able to control what happens to us; we can control what we do about it. You have more autonomy than you think. You may not be able to change your *circumstances*; you can change your *mindset*.

The Most Frequently Given Reasons for Why We Procrastinate

"Do you know the #1 prerequisite for change? A sense of urgency."

—JOHN KOTTER

Please take a moment to look over the reasons below that people give for *not* doing what they want. Which resonate with you?

1. **Time:** Are you waiting for more time, for the right time, to do what you want? What if that never happens? As John Legend said, "The future is already here and we're already late." Life Hack 5 shares ways to be happier in the moment, and they only take a moment.

2. **Money:** *CNN Money* reports, "78% of Americans say they live paycheck to paycheck. Six out of ten don't have $500 saved in the bank." Fortunately, being wealthy in what matters (chapter 17) doesn't have to cost a thing. For example, I was in a park yesterday watching a young couple with their toddler. They were blowing bubbles and having a grand time. I thought, "They could have paid thousands of dollars at a theme park and they wouldn't be having a better time than they're having for

free." As Garth Brooks says, "You aren't wealthy until you have something money can't buy."

3. **Family Responsibilities:** A woman told me, "I took a golden parachute deal from my company so I could retire early. What I didn't anticipate was both my parents would be diagnosed with dementia. I'm now a full-time caregiver. This is not how I envisioned spending my fifties." How about you? Are you so busy taking care of your kids, parents, coworkers, everyone else, that there's no time (or energy) left for you?

4. **Work Priorities:** A Gallup poll reports "72% of people are uninspired and unhappy at work, yet 52% don't take their full paid vacation." What's that about? Stanford professor Denise Brosseau told me, "In the Silicon Valley, it's almost a badge of honor to 'sleep under your desk.' Sixty-hour weeks are the norm." How about you? Is work running your life? At what cost?

5. **Health Challenges:** Are you dealing with aches and pains, a disability, an injury, or illness that is preventing you from doing what makes you happy? Or, are you taking your health for granted, promising yourself you'll get back into shape "Monday"?

6. **Fear of Change:** Change can be scary. You know what's scarier? Regrets. Chapter 8 shares a story of sailing the Chesapeake Bay and explores how you can be bold on your behalf. As Western writer Louis L'Amour said, "Nobody got anywhere in the world by simply being content."

7. **"I Don't Know What I Want."** A friend delivered the commencement address at her alma mater. The graduates took the stage for a group photo and, with a grand flourish, opened their robes to reveal T-shirts underneath that read: I DON'T KNOW. Sound familiar? It's hard to go after what we want if we *don't know* what we want. The next chapter can help you get crystal clear about a meaningful *Next* you can set in motion.

8. **Lack of Support from Significant Others:** Did you give up a dream or passion project because someone gave you grief about it and told you it was foolish or frivolous? Chapter 6 shows how

to say no to naysayers who are holding you back and causing you to question yourself.

9. **Resigned to Fate:** A coffee mug had this rather dismal slogan: "I know I'm not going to get what I want, so I'm not going to get my hopes up." A fifty-something man told me he was in a golden-handcuffs situation. When I asked him "What is something you're looking forward to?" he just gave me a blank expression. Yikes. As Theodore Roosevelt said, "It's far better to dare mighty things . . . than . . . to live in a gray twilight." The premise of this book is that life is to be *enjoyed*, not *endured*. Hack 5 shares specific ways to celebrate each and every day instead of existing in a "gray twilight."

It's Never Too Late—Or Too Early—to Change Things for Good

"Things don't get better by chance, they get better by change."
—JIM ROHN

Which of the above reasons did you relate to? Please understand, even if these reasons have been true for you in the past, they don't have to be true for you in the future.

One of the many wonderful things about being a human being is we can change for good—on any given day. All we have to do is identify *one thing* we're going to do differently and attach a sense of urgency to it so we're motivated to do it now, not in the far-off future.

Trish is an example of that. She told me she had moved to the Big Apple from the Midwest with stars in her eyes. Like many would be actor/singers before her, she had starred in school plays and community theater productions and dreamed of landing a role on Broadway. She said, "That was two years ago. I live in a tiny studio apartment and work as a waitress to pay bills. All I do in my spare time is go to one audition after another. I haven't had one call back. I'm so discouraged, I'm about to give up."

I asked her, "Have you heard about Daybreaker? It's a dance community that meets early in the morning at cool places around town—like on a cruise ship, in an art loft, or an open-air rooftop. It offers yoga, green juice, singing DJ's, and no wallflowers. Everyone's on their feet dancing to music. It beats staying home, alone in your room, getting depressed."

Trish didn't procrastinate. She registered for their next event and went. She got back in touch to say, "What a fun way to start the day. Early-bird tickets are only $20. Even I can afford that. You're right, everyone was so friendly. I can't believe I was on the brink of giving up and going home. Not only did I find my tribe, I've got something to look forward to every week."

I love Trish's story because it shows what can happen when we take responsibility for changing what we *can*. As an actor, her career success is not in her control. She can improve her craft and go to dozens of auditions, but that doesn't guarantee she'll land a role.

Instead of allowing that to define and defeat her, she did *one thing differently* to improve the quality of her life. I don't know the rest of Trish's story. I don't know if she ever got her big acting break. What I do know is she's happier now than she was. And isn't that what we all want?

Are You the Pilot or the Passenger of Your Life?

"The bad news is, time flies. The good news is, you're the pilot."
—MICHAEL ALTSCHULER

The challenge is, we can *want* to change, we can even know we *need* to change, but that doesn't necessarily mean we *will* change. Many of us resort to a lifelong default of sticking with our status quo. As John Kotter pointed out, it takes a sense of urgency for us to become the *pilot* of our life, not the *passenger*.

Our penchant for perpetual procrastination came up in the Q&A of a workshop in Waikiki.

Beverly said, "I've been to motivational programs before. I go home all fired up, then life intervenes, and two weeks later everything is back to same old, same old. Any suggestions?"

I told her, "Have a pretend S.E.E. to give yourself a sense of urgency. An S.E.E. is a Significant Emotional Event. Unfortunately, most are dramatic or traumatic. We get sick, divorced, or fired, and we are forced to reevaluate the way we're living. We realize there are no guarantees so we're motivated to focus on what matters *now* because we realize we may not get a second chance. The way I see it, why not have a *pretend* S.E.E. so we get the epiphany without the pain?"

"What's an example of a pretend S.E.E.?"

"We can do one right here, right now. Just ask yourself, "If I only had a week to live, what would I *stop* doing? What would I *start* doing? What would I *do differently?*"

"You're asking us to imagine we're going to croak in a week? Isn't that a little morbid?"

I smiled. "Thinking about our mortality isn't *morbid*; it's *motivating*. Sometimes it's just the incentive we need to stop taking our life, health, loved ones, and freedoms for granted."

She said, "Okay, I'll play along. If I only had a week to live, I would *stop* letting fear rule my life and *start* doing things that scare me."

"Like what?"

"Like going into the ocean. I watched the movie *Jaws* when I was a kid. Big mistake. Here I am in Hawaii and I haven't even gone into the water."

I said, "Okay, let's hack that fear. One way to hack fears is to realize they don't prevent things from going *wrong*; they prevent things from going *right*. Do you know about the protected swim area by the Natatorium where Duke Kahanamoku used to swim? It's only three-feet deep so there's no way you can get in over your head, and there's only one small opening in the sea wall so the surf can't get in . . . *and neither can the sharks*. Let's put a 'do date' on the calendar so you don't wiggle out of your intentions. When are you leaving the islands?"

"We fly out in two days."

"Then tomorrow is the day. Schedule a 6 a.m. wake-up call. When the alarm goes off and you're tempted to roll over and go back to sleep, ask yourself, 'What will matter a year from now? That I got an extra hour of sleep? Or that I finally overcame a fear that's been keeping me from living full out, and I got up and outside and had a one-of-a-kind experience I'll always be grateful for?'"

"It's worth a try. But why 6 a.m.?"

"Because sunrise is at 6:30 a.m. and you want to be at water's edge, ready to step into the ocean the moment the sun rises over Diamond Head. It will be what Hawaiians call a 'chicken skin' experience. Experiences are more meaningful when they're metaphors. You're not just stepping into the ocean, you're stepping into a new way of being where you remember your mortality and consciously take actions to make the most of your life now, not someday."

I added, "Here's my card with my number. Text me and let me know how it goes, okay?"

The next day Beverly texted "I DID IT!" with a smiley-face emoji.

What True Priority have you been postponing? Instead of vaguely promising you'll act on it *someday*, could you have a pretend S.E.E. to give yourself a sense of urgency so you're motivated to act on it *today*? If fears are holding you back, could you ask yourself, "What will matter a year from now?" Remind yourself, "Fears don't prevent things from going wrong; they prevent things from going right."

Chuck Yeager (the first pilot to break the sound barrier) said, "At the moment of truth, there are either reasons or results." In our next section, you'll learn more ways to turn reasons (aka excuses) into results (aka actions) by *generating* a mission or dream that gives purpose and meaning to your days.

LIFE HACK 2

GENERATE a Today, Not Someday Dream

"Tell me, what is it you plan to do with your one wild and precious life?"

—MARY OLIVER

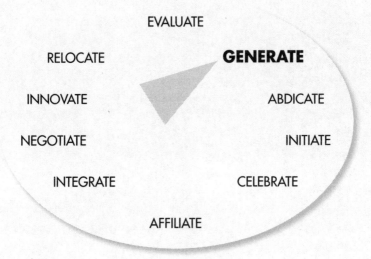

EVALUATE

RELOCATE   **GENERATE**

INNOVATE   ABDICATE

NEGOTIATE   INITIATE

INTEGRATE   CELEBRATE

AFFILIATE

Now that you've evaluated your happiness history and explored why you may have been postponing True Priorities, it's time to move on to the next Life Hack, which is how to GENERATE an inspiring dream or passion project that gives you a reason to wake up in the morning.

4

Clarify What You Want

"The question you should be asking isn't . . . 'What are
my goals?' but 'What would excite me?'"

—TIM FERRISS

A few weeks after finishing that Z-Pack for the walking pneumonia (which, thankfully, restored me to full health), I was driving along California's Highway 101 near Santa Barbara. I was on my way to present a public workshop at the Wilshire Country Club where Charlie Chaplin and Humphrey Bogart used to hang out. It was a gloriously sunny day, and I kept sneaking peeks over at the sun diamonds dancing on the ocean.

All of a sudden, a dream wanted to be born. You may be thinking, "A *what* wanted to be born?"

I know this may sound woo-woo but one of the most important takeaways from my seventeen years as Executive Director of the Maui Writers Conference was *"Ink it when you think it."* Our best-selling authors didn't agree on much but they did agree that when something pops into our head that wants to be said, *Write it down.* They're not called fleeting thoughts for nothing. If we don't jot thoughts when they're hot, they're gone, perhaps forever.

So, I pulled over, pulled out my ever-present pen and notebook, and *this* is what came out.

Some people are drawn to fire.

I am drawn to water.

After all, we are 65% water. Each of us, all of us, are bodies of water.

Yet water is a Maslow Hierarchy 'satisfied need.' As Maslow pointed out, satisfied needs are often ignored and overlooked. We tend to take them for granted.

Water wants a voice. Water needs a voice. Water deserves a voice. I will be that voice.

So it is, I will set out on my Year by the Water. (Side note: "My What?!")

On October 1, I will set out, travel around the country, and visit bodies of water. Oceans, rivers, lakes, waterfalls, mountain streams, and write about my reflections and realizations.

I will visit Sanibel Beach and find out if what Anne Morrow Lindberg said is true that "We can't pick up all the beautiful shells on the beach."

I will visit the river in Montana where the movie A River Runs Through It *was filmed and find out if it's true we can't step in the same river twice.*

I am clear that I am not supposed to control this trip. I am supposed to partner with what wants to happen, not plan every minute of it.

Like Charles Kuralt, I will interview interesting people along the way.

I will write about my adventures and insights in the hopes people find them inspiring.

And so it is.

Well! *That* was intriguing. I sat there, parked on the side of the road, blinking at the out-of-the-blue suddenness of it all. Where had this come from?

Who knows? But I'll always be grateful for this "divine intervention." I knew how rare it was to have a dream downloaded, with a name and start date no less. I understood what a gift it was to have a perfectly packaged *Next* delivered, verbatim, from "on high," that I was excited about.

My gratitude for this beat-the-odds confluence of events (more about that in chapter 10) caused me to be crystal clear that on October 1, I absolutely would be setting off for my Year by the Water. I didn't know exactly *how* I would do this, I just knew I would.

In case you're wondering, yes, I realized how fortunate I was to be in a position to do this. I was single and had autonomy. My kids were grown and on their own. My loved ones were all healthy so I wasn't a caretaker for any family members. I had a business I could take on the road to finance this. There was no one or no thing holding me back.

I called my sister, Cheri, who's been my business manager for twenty years, to share the news. Her response showed, once again, why I love her, trust her, and am so very grateful to work with her. She didn't question my sanity; she jumped in with, "Good for you. Let's make a list of what we need to do between now and September 30 to make this happen."

The perfect pragmatic, supportive response to move things forward. We had five months to, as Bono says, "dream out loud," and make arrangements for this transition. And that's what we did.

How about you? What is something that has been calling you? What is a long-delayed dream or passion project that could give meaning and momentum to your days?

What Gives Meaning and Purpose to Your Life?

"Happiness is when what you think, say, and do are in harmony."
— GANDHI

A twenty-something named Tyler told me, "Do you know how lucky you were to have a 'calling' downloaded to you? I don't know what I want to do for lunch, much less what I want to do next year or the year after that. The thing is, I don't even know where or how to start."

I told him, "It's ironic, isn't it? We're taught math, science, and history, but we're not taught how to lead a purposeful, meaningful life. Some of us are still trying to figure that out."

He said, "I agree with that, I just don't know what to do about it."

"I think it helps to create your own definition of happiness. When I ask people, 'What does happiness mean to you?' I often get long pauses and blank looks. If we can't define what happiness means to us, how are we supposed to know it when we experience it?"

I will always remember attending a conference breakout session on "The History of Happiness" presented by a professor who had written a book on the topic. He spent most of his sixty minutes quoting Aristotle, Socrates, and Plato. He left time for one question. The gentleman next to me raised his hand and said, "What's *your* definition of happiness?"

Deer in the headlights. He finally confessed he didn't have one. There was an audible gasp from the audience at his surprising revelation. The questioner wasn't about to let him off the hook. He said, "You've studied this topic for twenty years. Surely you have your own definition."

The professor realized he wasn't going to dodge the question and admitted, "Well, if I have to give a definition, I guess I'd agree with Stendahl who wrote, 'To describe happiness is to diminish it.'"

That was it. End of session. Wow. I turned to the man next to me and said, "I *so* disagree with that. I think defining and describing happiness helps us be more alert to it and appreciative of it."

He nodded in agreement. I asked, "When was the last time you were happy?"

He thought about it and then smiled, "My daughter called last week from her hospital to ask for my advice. She is a physician who's gone into my specialty of internal medicine. They had a seriously ill patient and hadn't been able to diagnose what was wrong. I asked her to list all his symptoms. I got a hunch based on what she told me and asked if they'd tested for a rather rare disorder. They hadn't. She called back the next day to let me know my hunch had been right. They'd started treatment, and it looked like they caught it in time and he would recover."

I told him, "*That's* happiness. To have an adult child who respects you enough to go into your profession, who seeks your advice which saves a life, and for the two of you to share that? Describing that experience doesn't *diminish* it, it *deepens* it."

How about you? When was a time you were deeply happy? Reenact it in your mind so you reexperience it. Who was there? What did they say? What helped make it a golden day?

Please note, happiness doesn't have to be "happy, happy, joy, joy." It doesn't have to look like Snoopy in the *Peanuts* cartoon strip, leaping into the air, clicking his heels (paws?), and doing a happy dance. What does happiness look like and feel like for you? Is it a quiet contentment? A peaceful recognition of what's right with your world? A satisfying connection with someone or something? This next exercise can help you get clear about what constitutes happiness for you.

What Does Happiness Mean to You?

"Someone asked what I regarded as the three most important requirements for happiness. My answer: A feeling you have been honest with yourself and those around you; a feeling you have done the best you could in your personal life and work; and the ability to love others."

— Eleanor Roosevelt

What are your three most important requirements of happiness? Can you integrate those into a one-sentence definition? Here are some samples to kick-start your thinking. Feel free to adapt these to create a definition that feels right to you.

To me, happiness means living in the moment and loving every moment.

To me, happiness means knowing I matter and being with people who matter.

To me, happiness means being my best possible self in all circumstances.

To me, happiness means to be in love and to be loved.

To me, happiness means making a positive difference for as many people as possible while leading a healthy, grateful life with friends and family. (That's mine.)

Okay, your turn. To me, happiness means _____

_____

See Happiness as a Skill and as a Choice

"What's dangerous is not to evolve."

—JEFF BEZOS

While creating your definition, you might also want to evolve your notion of happiness. It isn't just a *feeling* or a *result*; it is a *skill* and a *choice*. I've met famous high achievers who had every reason to be happy, yet they were miserable. At the same time, I know people facing grave challenges who are contentedly at peace with themselves and their life.

Glenna Salsbury, former President of the National Speakers Association, is a shining example of this. I just got off our monthly phone call. Everyone who has met Glenna, even for a few moments in the hall, describes her as a bright light who made them feel they were the most important person in the world. What many people don't know is she is dealing with Stage 4 cancer. Glenna's not having a pretend S.E.E. She's having a real S.E.E. She lives every day like it might be her last. That's not being trite; it's being true.

Glenna told me, "I had a good day yesterday. I felt good enough to get in the car and run errands. I remember going into the post office and thinking, 'I'm so happy. I'm so happy.'"

I said, "Glenna, you're dealing with 9-on-the-scale-of-10 pain. What made you so happy?"

"The simple things. I could drive. It was sunny. My girls love me. I just felt glad to be alive."

I asked, "What do you wish people knew that you now know?"

"I wish they would emotionally put themselves at the end of their life. It would help them be more *mindful* about how they spend their time."

"What do you mean?"

"Mindful is remembering that being alive is the ultimate gift. When we know we have a limited amount of time, we're more careful how we spend it. I ask myself every day, 'Does this *really* matter? What *will* matter in the long run?'"

Are You Treating Your True Priorities as an Afterthought?

"None of us are going to get out of here alive,
so please stop thinking of yourself as an afterthought."
— ANTHONY HOPKINS

Following our call, I reflected on Glenna's heartfelt wisdom and asked myself, "Am I honoring this gift of life? Am I being careful about how I'm spending my time? At the end of my days, what will I regret not doing and wish I had done?"

The answer came immediately. I would wish I had initiated more family outings. I've been fortunate this last year to spend time with my sons and their families at their respective homes. But it's been *three years* since we've all gotten together at the same time and place.

That's too long. I am the matriarch of our family. It is up to me to initiate gatherings. So, I sent everyone an email asking, "Who wants to do the Bolder Boulder 10K with me?"

The Bolder Boulder is the second-largest 10K in the country. Anyone can do it—competitive runners, walkers, babies in strollers, even corporate teams in costumes. This will give us something to train for and look forward to. It's a way to get fit and have fun while creating happy memories *together*. I can hardly put into words how *right* it feels to have set this in motion.

And look, it is in alignment with my definition of happiness, which is leading a healthy, grateful life with friends and family. It's a tangible way to match my Time Priorities with my True Priorities.

How about you? Are you spending your time carefully or carelessly? Are you treating your True Priorities as an "afterthought"? If you project yourself emotionally to the end of your life, what will you regret, what will you wish you had done? Why not initiate it now?

Margaret Bonnano said, "It's only possible to live happily ever after on a day to day basis." It's not too late to add meaning and purpose to your life. All you have to do is clarify a True Priority that will make you happier and then, as the next chapter shows, put a date on your calendar so you hold yourself accountable for doing it on a day-to-day basis.

5

Put a Date on the Calendar

"You don't have to see the whole staircase.
Just take the first step."

— MARTIN LUTHER KING, JR.

was lucky. My dream came with a start date. I couldn't see the whole staircase but I knew my first step. If there's anything I've learned about turning *Somedays* into *Todays* it's that a date on the calendar is the first step to making that dream come true. It is the key to turning an intangible wish into a tangible will.

I'm speaking from experience. Several years before, I awoke to the sound of cheers. I got up, looked out at my backyard lake, and realized it was the annual Jim McDonnell Lake Swim. I decided to walk my Jack Russell terrier (aka terror) over to check it out. Following an inspiring rendition of the "Star-Spangled Banner," the starter sent off the nationally ranked competitors and then the age groups: thirties, forties, fifties, sixties, seventies, eighty and above.

Eighty and above?! As I watched those fit octogenarians splash into the lake and take off for their mile-long race, I asked myself, "What's my excuse?!"

I used to be a competitive swimmer in high school and coached for a recreation league in Northern California. When I lived in Hawaii, I swam at dawn at Ala Moana Beach Park and competed in the 2.4-mile Waikiki Roughwater Swim. Here I was though, living on a lake and in a community with twelve pools, and sitting twelve hours a day as a desk potato. What makes this worse was I knew sitting is the new "cigarette smoking" and I was still doing it. No excuse!

This time, instead of simply telling myself I "should" get back into swimming, I walked home, jumped on the Waikiki Roughwater Swim website, and signed up on the spot.

The instant I registered, I became accountable. This was no longer a passing fancy; it was a commitment. I had to book flights/hotels, schedule training swims, and prepare for the race so I wouldn't embarrass myself when the big day came.

It turned into a family holiday. Tom served as land crew. Andrew decided to swim at the last minute (and beat me, the noogie). Longtime friends from Oahu and Kauai met me at the finish line on the beach at Hilton Hawaiian Village and we celebrated over Mai Tais.

If I hadn't put a date on the calendar and turned that intangible intention into a tangible commitment, none of that would have happened.

What's Your Start Date?

"Stop wearing your wishbone where your backbone ought to be."

—ELIZABETH GILBERT

So, what is a Someday you'd like to turn into a Today? When are you going to launch it? Putting a date on the calendar is a way to put your backbone where your wishbone is.

The importance of this is not just my opinion. A *New York Times* article by David DeSteno reports that "25 percent of all resolutions have fallen by the wayside by *January 8* of the new year." One reason we abandon our good intentions is we believe the key to keeping resolutions is to exercise willpower and self-control. The opposite is true. If we're already busy, tired and stressed, trying to discipline ourselves into being a better person can come across as more hard work. Who needs that?

Another reason we sometimes fail to make good on our resolutions is we focus on what we want to *stop* or *do less of,* which perpetuates the problem behavior because it keeps it top of mind.

Please understand, our mind can't focus on the opposite of an idea. It doesn't register the words "don't," "stop," "won't." If we say, "I *don't* want to eat *carbs*" or "I *won't* watch so much *TV,*" our mind registers the visual, emotionally charged words *"eat carbs"* and *"watch TV."*

If I'd told myself, "I've got to *stop* sitting so much," I would have perpetuated that bad habit.

That's why it's so important to eliminate "ghost" words and replace them with visual words that express your *desired* behavior and not the *dreaded* behavior. That means "I don't want to eat carbs" becomes "I love eating lean, green, and protein." "I won't watch so much TV" becomes "I spend Monday with my book club and Wednesday at church choir practice."

Doesn't that already sound that it's more likely to happen?

The More Specific You Get, the More Likely It Is to Happen

"Be brave enough to be your true self."

—QUEEN LATIFAH

An example of how using specific, positive language can increase the likelihood of getting our desired results unfolded at our first Someday Salon. I was in a small group with several people who were discussing what they'd put in Box 2 (Not Doing, Want To). Kimberly, a thirty-something woman, said, "The first thing I put down was *travel.* I took a gap year between high school and college. I got a Eurorail pass and toured Europe, staying in hostels and backpacking with people I met along the way. It was the best time of my life. I haven't traveled out of the country since I got a 'real job' ten years ago and I miss it."

I said, "Okay, let's get more specific. Travel where?"

She thought about it for a moment and then brightened as she thought of a place she had always wanted to visit. "Nepal."

"What do you want to do there? Trek the Himalayas?"

Her eyes brightened more as she started seeing this in her mind's eye. "Yes."

"All right, let's be more precise. Do you want to go by yourself or with a guided group?"

She started warming to the topic, "I want to go with an all-women's group."

The woman next to her said, "I know someone who did that. She had a fabulous time. She said it was the best gift she ever gave herself. What's your number? I'll text you her contact info."

When I moved on, they were animatedly discussing details of the trip. Her vague idea went from something she wrote in Box 2 to a specific dream that had already "come alive" in her mind.

That is the power of specifics. Want to turn your "I *wish*" into a "I *will?*" Fill in your W5 Form.

WHAT exactly do you want to do, see, experience? What resources do you need? What are next steps to making this happen?

_____

_____

WHY does this light you up? Why is this something meaningful you would enjoy? _____

WHERE specifically do you want to go? _____

_____

WHEN would you go? _____

_____

WHO would you go with? Who can you contact to move this forward? _____

_____

The more W's you picture for your project, the more "real" it becomes in your mind's eye because it turns something vague into something visual and visceral.

Pearl S. Buck said, "Stories were full of hearts broken by love, but what really broke a heart was taking away its dream, whatever that dream might be."

What takes away a dream is not committing a date to it on your calendar. If you want your dream to come true, post your W5 Form—*What? Why? When? Where? Who?*—where you'll see it every day. The more detailed you get, the more invested you are, and the most invested you are, the more likely it is your dream will come true.

Now that you've clarified what happiness means to you, and what you would look forward to, the next section will help you to clear away anything that might be in your way.

LIFE HACK 3

ABDICATE Outdated Beliefs and Behaviors

"You can't have everything. Where would you put it?"
— GEORGE CARLIN

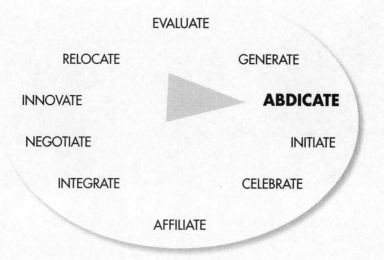

Now that you've EVALUATED your happiness history and GENERATED a meaningful dream to give your life purpose, it's time to abdicate non-essentials. The word ABDICATE means to "disown, relinquish, give up." That's exactly what we need to do with physical and emotional stuff that might be taking up time, energy, and resources that could be used for higher priorities.

6

Just Say No to Naysayers

> "Don't let them tame you."
>
> —Isadora Duncan

I was so excited about my Year by the Water, I decided to announce it at a National Press Club salon. What I didn't anticipate was the less-than-supportive reaction from a few attendees.

When I shared (what I thought was) my good news, most of the group cheered and broke into spontaneous applause. Several called out, "Take me with you!"

However, a few guests were less supportive. One pulled me aside and asked with grave concern, "Are you okay?"

Taken aback, I told her, "Yes, why do you ask?"

She didn't come right out and say it, but I realized she had come to the conclusion I must be on my deathbed to make such a "drastic change."

I reassured her, "I'm not having a midlife *crisis*. I'm having midlife *clarity*."

Another said, "Gee, must be nice. Wish I could take a year-long vacation." He seemed to be implying I was, as the lyrics in the Cyndi Lauper song go, "just a girl who wants to have fun."

A management consultant told me, "You know, part of me envies you, but the other part of me would go crazy doing *nothing*." He continued, "Sam, you need to control this story. If word gets out you're off the grid and you fall off your clients' radar, you may not have a business to come home to. Are you sure you want to put everything you worked so hard for at risk? You know, you can't put the genie back in the bottle."

Hmm. It's true that I was looking forward to having fun. And I guess it was true this was a drastic change. But it wasn't true that I was going to do "nothing." It wasn't true there was something desperately "wrong" with my life I was trying to escape. And I hoped it wasn't true that I needed to hide this venture from my clients lest they lose respect for me, or interest in me.

Little could I have predicted that singer James Taylor would come to the rescue and provide a "frame" for these issues. I was watching *CBS Sunday Morning* and a reporter asked Taylor, "You just released a new album, your first in twelve years. What took so long?"

Taylor explained that he needed time and space to compose new music and that he'd been busy touring. The reporter said, "So, you took time off work to write?"

Taylor thought about it for a moment and then said, "I didn't take time *off* work; I did a *different kind* of work."

Ahh. The perfect frame for my Year by the Water. I wasn't taking time *off* work; I was doing a *different kind* of work. I wasn't doing *nothing*; I was doing *something* that thrilled me every time I thought about it.

How about you? Did you announce your intention to launch your project and someone rained on your parade? Did you tell a significant other you were going to learn a new skill or pick up an old passion, and instead of supporting you, they told you all the reasons it wouldn't work?

How has that impacted you? Did you allow yourself to be talked out of your dream? Did you give up what you wanted to do because this person yanked the confidence carpet out from underneath your feet?

Be Your Own Champion

"No one can figure out your worth but you."

— PEARL BAILEY

If you are receiving push-back to your project that is undermining your resolve to do more of what's important to you, it is crucial to find and align with people who believe in you. In fact, the more people, the better. Research shows that a primary predictor of successful habit change is whether you're hanging with encouraging peers who share and support your goals.

As you can imagine, there's an app for that.

Xander Schultz, CEO of Complete Labs, says their research shows that when people abandon their goals, it's not always for lack of *inspiration*; it's for lack of *accountability*. "They know what they want and need to do, but there isn't that extra kick in the butt to complete it."

In other words, if you want to stand strong and persevere through challenges, it's important to reach out to people instead of retreat and withdraw from people.

In fact, a 2013 study published in *Translational Behavioral Medicine* reports that participants who published their weight-loss progress on Twitter lost more weight than those who were quiet about their progress. There's a good reason for this. Not only are we more answerable when we have an audience, the incoming encouragement ramps up our enthusiasm.

That's what happened to me.

In one of those lucky coincidences (more about those in chapter 10), the day after I watched that interview with James Taylor, I discovered he was playing a concert in the area. I bought two tickets and called a friend to see if she wanted to go with me.

She agreed on the spot, which is how I found myself on a much-welcomed drive to and from Hershey, Pennsylvania, with my friend Lee Self.

Lee organizes mastermind groups for executives. I recounted the advice given me about the "dangers" of going off the grid and asked, "Do you think I should keep my adventure quiet?"

She said, "Sam, give your clients credit. I think they'll be happy for you. You're the one who taught me that people can't jump on our bandwagon if it's parked in the garage. As long as you make it clear you're not closing your business forever, that you're still speaking and consulting, I think they'll support you and want to be kept in the loop."

Lee was right. I announced my Year by the Water in our next newsletter, and Cheri and I were overwhelmed, in a good way, by an outpouring of generous invitations. "I have a houseboat in Sausalito. You can stay there." "Come to Whidbey Island. We'll write and watch the eagles."

I'll always be grateful to James Taylor and to Lee Self for reminding me that the people who want the best for us are usually happy for us when we launch a passion project.

Since then, if a naysayer insists on pointing out all the things that might go wrong with something I'm planning, I ask myself, "What's their intent? Do they have my best interests at heart—or do they have a hidden agenda that is more about them than me?"

Time and again, true friends show up, pitch in, and go above and beyond to help our dreams come true. We'll get more specific about how to find and align with people who have your back (and front) in Life Hack 6: AFFILIATE. For now, let's return to what you can do if someone is trying to talk you out of your dream.

What to Do When Someone Is Raining on Your Parade

"Sometimes people try to destroy you, precisely because they recognize your power. Not because they don't see it, but because they see it and they don't want it to exist."

—BELL HOOKS

A woman from Australia named Wendy said, "You've heard of the 'tall poppy syndrome'? That's when someone 'cuts you down to size' because they're jealous or possessive. They don't want you to be bigger than them.

I've got someone like that in my life. Every time I think of trying something new, he tears it down and then adds, 'I'm telling you this for your own good.' I wish there were a way to know if he really does have *my* best interests at heart or whether he has *his* best interests at heart."

I told Wendy, "There are ten questions you can ask to get clarity about whether someone is telling you something for *your* own good or for *their* own good. Answering these questions can help you determine whether a naysayer in your life is what I call a 5 percenter. Ninety-five percent of people want to cooperate and want a win-win. five percenters want to control and want to win. Five percenters knock you down to keep you small because they see your happiness as a threat. They're afraid if you do something you love, you'll leave them. They don't care what's fair, they want to keep you theirs. If after answering these questions, this person clearly has a pattern of putting you down to keep you down, it would be wise to remove that person from your life or remove yourself from theirs.

The Clarity Quiz When Dealing with Naysayers

> "When someone shows you who they are,
> believe them the first time."
>
> —MAYA ANGELOU

Please think of a person in your life who seems to put obstacles in your path whenever you share something that is important to you. What is this person doing or saying that discourages you or causes you to question yourself? Now ask yourself these questions.

1. Is this person aware that what they're doing is undermining your confidence? Are they just spouting an opinion or this is a deliberate campaign to derail you?
2. Is it this person's "nature" to be cautious and careful? Do they think it is their role or responsibility to "look out for you" and save you from danger or risk?

3. Is this a one-time incident or an ongoing issue? Does this person have a pattern of trying to "hold back," or is their input specific to this particular situation?

4. Have you told this person how you feel? When you told this person how their behavior is affecting you, did they genuinely listen to you or talk over you and brush you off?

5. Is it possible that you're not listening to them? Could these be valid concerns you need to take into consideration? Do you need to give their input a chance vs. shutting it down?

6. Could there be extenuating circumstances you may not be taking into account? Is their behavior driven by a fear or protectiveness that explains it—even if it doesn't excuse it?

7. Is there an objective third party who can help you get perspective about this? Someone who is not emotionally invested who could give you wise, objective counsel?

8. Play out what would happen if you heed this person's warnings and *don't do* what you want to do. Is it possible you would thank them in the long run? Or would you feel defeated and deflated, as if you'd abandoned a dream that was meaningful to you?

9. Now play out how you would feel if you proceed with your plans. Would you look back and see this as a hasty, impulsive decision you wish you had thought through more rigorously? Or, would you be glad you bet on yourself and honored your gut instincts?

10. Is it worth trying to have an honest, two-way conversation with this person or are they locked into their point of view? Will it do any good to try to resolve this situation with them or is it wiser to move on and connect with people who will help move this forward?

Alice Walker said, "No person is your friend who . . . denies your right to grow." What did you conclude after asking yourself these questions? Is this person trying to help you grow or do they see your growth as a threat?

If you've concluded this person's goal is to keep you under their thumb, you might want to follow Gertrude Stein's advice, "Let me listen to me, not to them," and proceed with your passion project instead of letting them derail it.

For now, let's move on and see what else you might want to abdicate what could be holding you back from the quality of life you want, need, and deserve.

7

Let It Go, Let It Go, Let It Go

"The most important things in life aren't things."

— Ann Landers

Have you seen George Carlin's brilliant YouTube rant on "stuff"? While flying over a city, he looks down and sees thousands of buildings, all with *stuff* inside. He riffs on the amount of time, money, and energy it takes to buy that stuff, clean that stuff, move that stuff, repair that stuff. He observes, "A house is just a place to keep your stuff while you go out and get more stuff. If you have to buy more stuff to store your stuff, maybe you have too much stuff."

As the saying goes, "First we own our possessions, then they own us."

Are your possessions contributing to your quality of life or are they just *things* that won't really matter in the long run? Is all that stuff consuming time, energy, and money you would rather be spending on something more rewarding?

I'm here to tell you that getting rid of 95 percent of my stuff—and this included some very nice stuff—was one of the most freeing things I've ever done. Yet I might not have been able to let it go, let it go, let it go, if it weren't for Mary LoVerde. She was the one who convinced me there are more important things than things. She had been there, done this. She had walked into her "dream home" several years before, the home she had built from scratch and raised her family in, and a voice told her, "All the reasons you created this home are complete. Go."

As she likes to say, the voice didn't tell her *where* to go, she guessed she was supposed to figure that out along the way. She was clear she didn't want to have a yard/estate sale. She had invested a lot of care into selecting "just right" items for each room. She wanted the satisfaction of knowing that her things would be enjoyed by people she cared for. She wasn't interested in haggling over prices with strangers.

So Mary invited twenty longtime friends to an "open house." She gave each person Post-it notes to place on the items of their choice with the agreement they would be removed within the week. Voilà. Seven days later, Mary had given away most of what she owned to people who valued it and promised to put it to good use. A win for all involved.

So when Mary came to my home to help me "clean house" and right-size my possessions in preparation for my Year by the Water, she knew the right questions to ask.

And the questions weren't, "How can I give that away?! Do you know how much that cost?!" The five "Shall I Take It, Store It, or Donate It?" questions were:

+ Do I actively use or wear this?
+ Would someone else appreciate it more than me?
+ Will this fit into my car and will I need/use it on the road in the coming months?
+ Does this deserve to sit in a POD for a year or two or more?
+ Does the person who gave me this—or created this—really care if I keep it?

I followed Mary's example. Instead of trying to sell things on Craigslist or have an estate sale, I donated pretty much everything. The only things I kept were tax records, meaningful gifts from the boys, and my one-of-a-kind writing desk that has played such an important role in my life.

In the beginning, I would look at an expensive piece of furniture and think, "I can't give *that* away." Mary would gently ask the five questions which reminded me why I wanted to go minimalist.

What I could not have anticipated was how much joy it gave me to give stuff away. That expensive kayak? You should have seen the smile on my friend's face when I gifted it to her. That matched dining and bedroom set was a well-deserved thank you to a woman who cleaned my home for twelve years. The business suits went to Dress for Success. It made me happy to know some deserving women may land the job of their dreams because they had professional attire that boosted their confidence and matched their new employer's expectations.

And you know what? Three years later? I don't miss *any* of that stuff. None of it.

Is It Time to Right-Size Your Life?

"In the scope of a happy life, a messy desk or overstuffed closet may seem trivial, yet I find . . . getting rid of clutter gives a disproportionate boost to happiness."

—GRETCHEN RUBIN

How about you? Is it time to clean house? Could clearing away non-essentials free up bandwidth that could give a disproportionate boost to your happiness?

A young woman, Carol, told me, "I read Marie Kondo's book *The Life-Changing Magic of Tidying Up*. It lived up to its title because it really did change my life."

"How so?"

"Well, I followed her advice to take it a little bit at a time. Instead of being overwhelmed by the stacks and piles, I just took it drawer by drawer. Each time I picked something up, I asked myself, "Is it beautiful, functional, or meaningful?" If it was, I put it back when I was finished with it. If it wasn't, I put it in a laundry basket to take to Goodwill or the trash basket if I was throwing it out."

"How did that affect your quality of life?"

"For the first time in a long time, I look forward to coming home. I used to feel guilty just walking in the door because there was stuff everywhere. Marie talks in her book about how *good* a clean house makes you feel and it's true. I look around now and everything just feels *right*."

A woman in the same workshop said, "I read Marie's book too but it impacted me differently."

"In what way?"

"I couldn't stop thinking about her comment that the things in our home are supposed to *spark joy*. There wasn't a lot of joy in my home. In fact, there wasn't much joy in my life."

"What was going on?"

"I work in the city but, at that time, lived in the suburbs because it was the only place I could afford a home. It was an hour's commute each way. If there was an accident or bad weather, that doubled. I was gone by dawn and usually didn't get home until after dark."

"So, how did Marie's book motivate you to change?"

"It made me rethink my whole life. Why was I working so hard to pay for a house I was never in? What I put in Box 2 (not doing) was have a social life. What I put in Box 3 (what I was doing I didn't want to) was commuting. People at work would ask me out for a drink or invite me to an event in town but I always said no because it meant getting home so late."

"So, what helped you reach critical mass?"

"I was complaining to a coworker about how much I dreaded my daily commute. She told me a friend was selling his apartment in the building she lives in and asked if I wanted to stop by after work to see it. I thought, 'Why not? It can't hurt.'

"The minute I walked in, I knew I'd found my new home. It's half the size of my old place, but I wasn't using all that extra space anyway so why was I paying for it? What's even better is there is a Metro stop two blocks from the building and it only takes me fifteen minutes to get to and from my office. Not only do I not have to worry about tolls, parking, and traffic every day, I get home at a decent hour and have all kinds of options right outside my front door. After all these years, I finally have a social life!"

Say Good-Bye to What's Weighing You Down and Hello to What Lifts You Up

"If you're brave enough to say good-bye,
life will reward you with a new hello."

— PAULO COELHO

Are you thinking, "Well, it sounds like those ladies live by themselves so they can make these unilateral decisions. I have a spouse (or kids or roommates) and don't have that luxury."

I hear you. It's one thing to "clean house" if you live alone; it's another thing if you live with people who want to stay put or who don't care how cluttered the house is.

You and your significant others might want to watch the TED talk given by Graham Hill called "Less Stuff, More Happiness." He introduces some jaw-dropping statistics in his talk; e.g., we have three times as much space as we did fifty years ago but it's still not enough for all our stuff. The personal storage industry is a $24 billion industry. In fact, there are more self-storage facilities in the United States than Starbucks, McDonald's, and Subway combined!

Yet, the majority of people never even visit their storage unit, much less take out and use what they stashed away. Do the math. If you're paying $125 a month (the national average) to store stuff you don't use, that tallies up to $1,500 a year. Wouldn't you rather have the cash?

And in case you're wondering what this has to do with your happiness, ask yourself how you spend your weekends and evenings. Do you spend it doing household and yard chores? Do you spend it shopping and buying more stuff you'll need to take care of? Do you work long hours to make money to pay for stuff you're never home to enjoy? If so, now is the time to start abdicating some of that stuff so you're free to focus on what's genuinely signficant to you.

Just Say No to Stuff that Fills Your Life but Not Your Soul

"Knowing what you want out of life, and who you want in it, means nothing if you can't also say no to everything but those people and things. Until you cultivate the ability to say no to the things that fill your life but not your soul, you'll never have the space to bring into it the things you desperately want to say yes to."

—JONATHAN FIELDS

I asked psychologist Dianne Gerard, "Why do we do this to ourselves? Why do we spend so much time acquiring things when we know in our hearts it doesn't really lead to happiness?"

She told me, "Shopping can be an addiction. Some people go to the mall for something to do. It's their recreation and entertainment. Once they're there, the stores' seductive merchandising tempts them to buy things because it's a temporary high and makes them (temporarily) feel good. It's a mood-changer that relieves boredom, is pleasurable, and is momentarily gratifying.

"For some people, being surrounded by belongings feels like a security blanket. It relieves anxiety because they look around and think, 'I have everything I need.' That's why it can be tough to get rid of stuff. They think, 'What if I need it and don't have it anymore?' That causes unease so they hoard old magazines, clothes, books, etc. just in case they need them *someday*."

I could talk all day about the metaphorical lessons I learned while Mary and I went through each room deciding, "What stays? What goes?" Even though my sons had been out of the house for years, I had saved their stuff *just in case*. Tom's room had floor-to-ceiling shelves packed with hardback books. Think about it. Most of those books cost $20 to $25 new and there were hundreds of books. I called and asked Tom, "Do you want me to ship them, store them, what?"

There was a long pause. Then he said, "*Well, I forgot I had them, so I guess I don't need them.*"

Mary kept reminding me of that every time I was reluctant to let something go. Her motto was, "If you can video it or take a photo of it, you don't need to keep it." So, I did an oral video history of Tom's and Andrew's school projects. I video'd a little story about each book clients have given me and then donated them to my local library so they're out in the world reaching new readers instead of being stashed in a dark POD where they can't do anyone any good.

I'll say it again. I am grateful to have owned those things and for the role they played in contributing to my life, but I don't miss any of them. Letting them go freed me to go. I would not have had these global adventures if I was still house-bound. The energy I feel for my life is a direct result of lightening my load and not having roomfuls of things I need to take care of.

Collect Experiences, Not Objects

"Clutter is not just the stuff on your floor . . . it's anything that stands between you and the life you want to be living."."

— Peter Walsh

A client told me, "There's another reason to get rid of our stuff sooner, not later. I collect embroidered handkerchiefs and original oyster plates. It's been a rewarding hobby over the years and I'm considered an expert on the art and business of collecting.

"The only problem? Times have changed and so have values. Many of my clients planned to pass along their collections but their kids don't want them. Even when they're worth a lot of money—we're talking fine crystal, silverware, antiques—the younger generation is saying, 'No thanks.'"

I told her, "I saw an article by Tom Verde in *The New York Times* titled 'Aging Parents with Lots of Stuff and Children Who Don't Want It.' The gist of it was millennials are minimalists, not materialists; they don't care about inheriting their mom's gravy boat or their grandparents' china."

She sighed, "I could tell you heartbreaking stories about seniors who were devastated to discover their kids had no interest in their heirlooms. It's smarter to get ahead of that instead of being emotionally blindsided by it when it's time to move to an assisted living facility."

"So, what do you suggest?"

"By all means, continue collecting things if it makes you happy. Just make provisions to donate those things to a museum or sell them to another collector when the time comes. Otherwise, collect experiences, not objects. Ask your kids what they want from you. Chances are they prefer shared memories now instead of material stuff later.

"You might also want to hire someone to help. There are services that do a door-to-door cleaning, conduct an estate sale, and take remaining items of value to a consignment shop. Their fee comes out of the revenue that's produced. Many clients who have felt guilty for putting this off tell me what a relief it is to have this taken care of instead of looming over their heads."

Barbara Hemphill, former president of the National Association of Professional Organizers, says, "Clutter is simply delayed decisions."

Don't delay. Google organizations in your area *today* to find one that can help you clear away clutter that is clogging your life. Put a date on the calendar right now when you'll start abdicating things you *don't want* to free up time, space, and money for the life you *do want*.

The next chapter isn't about abdicating *things*, it's about abdicating *thinks*. In particular, default beliefs that could be undermining your happiness that you might not even be aware of.

8

Stop Driving into Hurricanes

"Life has no remote. You have to get up and
change it yourself."

—Unattributed Pinterest post

Finally. October 1. Launch day for my Year by the Water. Friends hosted a send-off party at my favorite restaurant. What a joy it was looking around the table at my friends, some of whom I've known for thirty years, and sharing plans for my upcoming adventure. They were eager to hear all the details. "What's your first stop?"

"The Chesapeake Bay. I'm going to a friend's vacation home for a week to write."

"Where after that?"

"Not too sure."

"Really? You haven't mapped out your route?"

"Nope, I'm clear that I'm supposed to make it up as I go along."

"Well, whatever you do, keep an eye out for that hurricane."

"Hurricane?!" I had been so busy making trips to Goodwill and cleaning the house, I hadn't been watching the news or weather reports and had no idea what she was talking about.

"Yes, there's a hurricane on its way up the East Coast."

"Well! I better get on the road and get ahead of it."

An hour later, I was driving through horizontal rain with my windshield wipers valiantly trying to keep up. I peered ahead, trying to keep my car on the road. All of a sudden, a thought bubble appeared above my head, "*Why drive into a hurricane?*"

Well, I have promises to keep and miles to go before I sleep. Right? I was taught to keep my commitments—no matter what. We do what we say we're going to do. But this was scary and unsafe. Maybe under the circumstances, it would be okay, even advisable, to break a promise?

I pulled over and called my friend. "Laura, I'm sorry to back out but the weather's getting worse. Okay if I take you up on your offer another time?"

She didn't even hesitate. "Good call. You're welcome to visit another time. Stay safe."

It's hard to put into words the relief that washed over me. I found a nearby B & B on Expedia, and an hour later was nestled under a warm down comforter, glad to be off the road, safe and sound instead of battling the storm.

The next morning, I got up, walked outside, strolled the streets of Annapolis and discovered the Chris Deli, home of the best crab omelets in the universe. I scored a table, ordered my breakfast, and sang along with their traditional playing of the "Star-Spangled Banner."

I reflected on what had happened the night before. It was the first time in a long time I had broken a commitment. Yet it didn't feel *wrong*, it felt *right*. Maybe I needed to rethink my default that we keep commitments—no matter what.

Where else was I automatically keeping commitments because I thought—and had been taught—it was the "right thing" to do? Where else was I honoring arrangements made long ago that were no longer viable? Where else was I driving into hurricanes because I said I would?

What Commitments Are You Keeping Only Because You Said You Would?

"I'm no longer accepting the things I cannot change.
I am changing the things I cannot accept."
— ANGELA DAVIS

A friend told me that "Why drive into a hurricane?" has become a "go to" phrase in her family. When she or one of her kids is about to head into a stormy situation, they stop and ask themselves, "Am I driving into a hurricane? Why? Is there a better alternative?"

If we know we're heading into a hot mess, and doing it out of duty, tradition, or misplaced loyalty, maybe it's wise *not to do it*. Maybe there's another route that's a win for all involved. Sometimes it's not rude to opt out of a commitment; it's the right thing to do. It can even be in everyone's best interests to revisit and renegotiate a promise that is no longer practical.

A bookkeeper said, "I'm having a hard time with this. I understand what you're saying in principle, but in business, keeping commitments is the basis of courtesy, credibility, and honorability. The only way our customers and coworkers can trust us is if they know they can count on us to do what we agreed to do. I deal with financial records and contracts. Honoring commitments is a matter of *law*."

I told her, "You're right, when there is a written contract, we are legally bound to honor it. Please understand, it was drummed into me from an early age that keeping commitments was a nonnegotiable. We did what we said we'd do. Period. No excuses. No exceptions."

That's why I was driving into that hurricane, and that's why it was such a revelation to realize that maybe, just maybe, I didn't have to. This experience, and the fact that the home owner was glad I changed my mind, opened my eyes to the fact that doing what we've said we're going to do—no matter what—is not always optimal or necessary, given new information.

Please understand, I'm not suggesting we back out of commitments just because they've become inconvenient or because we don't feel like doing them anymore. What I'm suggesting is that we explore alternatives if keeping a commitment means putting our well-being at risk.

My friend asked, "What's an example?"

"Here's one. A young couple said the question 'Are we driving into a hurricane?' helped them reclaim their family holidays, which had turned into a nightmare over the years. The husband's parents lived in the Northeast in a not-kid-friendly home so they were constantly on alert to keep their toddlers out of the electrical plugs, off the fine furniture, and away from the balconies.

"Two of his uncles had radically different political views and one had a drinking problem. It was usually only a matter of time before everyone was off their best behavior and arguing. On top of all this, it was expensive to fly at peak season. They'd been doing it for years out of a sense of familial duty but wondered if enough was enough and there might be a better way.

"Her mom helped them come up with that better way. She suggested, 'Why don't you propose they join you over spring vacation at your time-share?' She pointed out that they'd have more "private time" at a kid-friendly place where there's plenty for everyone to do. They'd save money because it was off-season and no one would have to worry about political arguments or the kids tracking in mud on the white carpet."

"It was a win all the way around. At first his parents were 'hurt' the kids weren't coming home for the holidays (Everyone else will be there! It's a tradition!), but the couple was clear this was a happier, healthier option compared to those 'hurricane holidays.'"

What situation are you dealing with that isn't working for you anymore? Could you have a "Tell the truth as fast as you can" conversation with this person to determine if it's really necessary to keep this commitment or whether there are options neither of you have considered?

Who knows? Maybe they'll agree it's time for a change. Maybe, together, you can come up with an agreement that benefits both of you. The goal is to abdicate locked-in beliefs or arrangements that are sabotaging your well-being instead of supporting it.

Part of your happiness depends on your willingness to have honest conversations instead of continuing to do the same old, same old. In Life Hack 8—NEGOTIATE—you'll learn specific ways to speak up for what you want, need and believe so you're comfortable doing this.

For now, it's time to abdicate another outdated belief—that our ducks need to be in a row to go.

INITIATE Daily Actions That Move Your Life Forward

"You have got to own your days and live them, each one of them, every one of them, or else the years go by and none of them belong to you."

—HERB GARDNER

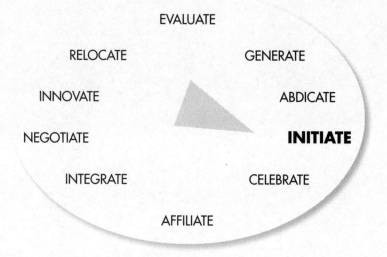

EVALUATE

RELOCATE   GENERATE

INNOVATE   ABDICATE

NEGOTIATE   **INITIATE**

INTEGRATE   CELEBRATE

AFFILIATE

Now that you've abdicated some things that might have been pre-venting you from pursuing more purposeful activities, Life Hack 4—INITIATE—shows a variety of ways to get out of inertia, be bold on our own behalf and own your days so your years belong to you. You'll learn why you don't have to be courageous; you just have to trust you can figure things out along the way.

9

You Don't Have to Know to Go

"I have learned, as a rule of thumb, never to ask whether you can do something. Say, instead, that you _are_ doing it. Then fasten your seat belt. The most remarkable things follow."

—JULIA CAMERON

t was Mother's Day and I was in Annapolis with an open day. I went downstairs and asked the hotel concierge, "Any suggestions?"

"What do you like to do? Shop? Visit historical sites? Sample our great local seafood?"

"It's a beautiful spring day. I'd love to do something active outside."

"Then you've got to go for a sail with Captain Jen. She operates a charter out of the harbor. Let me see if she's got any openings this afternoon."

She did. That's how I found myself sailing Chesapeake Bay on her 74-foot classic schooner, the _Woodwind_. If you're into boats, she's the beauty that was featured in the movie _Wedding Crashers_. Remember the family yacht they took out for a sail? Well, this was _that_ boat.

There were about twenty of us on board, people of all ages. Captain Jen finished her friendly, instructive orientation with "It's a great day to be on the bay." Indeed it was. A few minutes after motoring out of the harbor, she called out the favorite words of any sailor, "Power off, sails up."

The wind filled the sails and the boat lifted, heeled, and dug in, all at the same time. It was, in a word, *uplifting*. Captain Jen saw how thrilled I was and asked, "Want to take the helm?"

Would I like to take the helm?! I stood up, placed my hands at the 10 and 2 position and begin the delicate balance of pointing toward a buoy halfway to the horizon, adapting to the boats around us, and leveraging the wind to keep the sails right and tight.

If you've sailed before, you know there are times when all the elements come together and everything feels gloriously right with your world. This was that day.

Jen and I started talking and I shared some of my Year by the Water adventures. She said, "I'm curious. Of everything that's happened, what's surprised you the most?"

I thought about it then said, "That people think it's *brave*. The irony is, I've never once thought of this as being brave."

She laughed and said, "That's how I feel! People think starting and running my own charter is courageous but I see it as fun. I think it's because of the way I was brought up. My parents were both music teachers. We spent every summer on a sailboat. I remember them giving me five dollars and sending me into town in a little dinghy to 'get some ice cream.'"

She laughed and said, "It wasn't until later I realized that was more about them getting privacy than it was about me getting ice cream. The thing was, they didn't caution me to be careful or warn me about all the things that could go wrong when they sent me off in that dinghy. They were confident I could handle anything that came up, so I did."

I told her, "The same thing happened to my sister and me, except with horses. We lived in a small town that had more horses than people. Even when we were eight and nine years old, we would be gone all day and our folks never worried about us. To put this in perspective, this was before cell phones; they didn't even know where we were. But instead of worrying, they trusted that if anything happened, we'd figure it out. If my horse's bridle broke, figure it out. If my horse ran away with me, figure it out. We got good at being resourceful."

Jen said, "My folks were the same way. You know what that taught me? To be independent, self-sufficient, and to see the world as an adventurous place, not a scary place."

How about you? Do you see the world as an adventurous place or as a dangerous place? Do you see venturing out on your own as exciting or scary? When considering something new, do you worry about all the things that could go wrong or trust you can figure them out if they do?

Courage Is Just Trusting You Can Figure Things Out Along the Way

"Life expands or contracts in proportion to our courage."
— ANAÏS NIN

That discussion with Captain Jen stayed with me because people on my travels kept asking how I got the courage to do this on my own. I decided to dig deeper into why I embraced this adventure without fear. Once I decided to go, I was raring to go. No anxiety, just excitement.

Why?

I realized there was another pivotal event that prepared me to "take the helm." When it was time to choose a college major, I couldn't make up my mind. Counselors were advising me to be a doctor or lawyer, to "use my brain." But I wanted to study Recreation Administration. I had competed in sports since I was seven years old and thought running community recreation programs would give me a chance to do work I enjoyed that mattered.

But I was getting a lot of pushback. An uncle put his hands up in mock horror when he heard I was considering Rec Admin as my major. "What?! You're going to take classes in Underwater Basket weaving?!" Yes, he actually said that. Several other adults told me this was a "slacker degree" and advised me to challenge myself with a more rigorous major like law or medicine.

I will always be grateful to my dad for putting this in perspective. One night at dinner, he handed me a copy of this quote from W. H. Murray and followed it with: "Sam, when you need to make a decision and don't know what to do, go with your gut and take the bolder of the options."

> "Until one is committed, there is hesitancy, the chance to draw back. Concerning all acts of initiative (and creation), there is one elementary truth, the ignorance of which kills countless ideas and splendid plans: that the moment one definitely commits oneself, then Providence moves too. All sorts of things occur to help one that would never otherwise have occurred. A whole stream of events issues from the decision, raising in one's favor all manner of unforeseen incidents and meetings and material assistance, which no man could have dreamed would have come his way. Whatever you can do, or dream you can do, begin it. Boldness has genius, power, and magic in it. Begin it now."
>
> —W. H. MURRAY

These were the right words at the right time. Murray's wisdom (the last two lines are often attributed to Goethe) gave me the courage to choose what felt right for me—even though there were no guarantees it would turn out well. My heart was saying, "Recreation lights you up. You don't know if it's the *right thing* to do, but it is what *resonates* with you."

So, I made what I now call a "Congruent Decision at a Crucial Crossroads." I went with what felt right. I've never looked back and never regretted that decision. In fact, I've come to understand we never regret taking bolder options that are congruent with our voice, vision, and values. Our gut is the best moral compass of what to do when we don't know what to do.

In ways I couldn't have predicted at the time, choosing to study what "felt right" became the first stepping-stone in an aligned life where the light is on in my eyes.

When There Are No Guarantees—Go with Your Gut

> "We always experience anxiety whenever
> we confront the potential of our own development."
> —Søren Kierkegaard

Are you thinking, "Well, good for you. But what does that have to do with me?"

Several things. The first is, are you facing a big decision and not sure what to do? Do you have several options and no clarity? Are you getting conflicting advice about your next steps?

Remember W. H. Murray's wisdom. Nothing good comes from indecision. And nothing good comes from following other people's advice when it flies in the face of your values and vision. It is time to take the helm of your life. The very act of deciding in favor of what feels right will move things forward and give Providence (or whatever you want to call it) a chance to jump on your bandwagon. But that won't happen if your bandwagon stays in the garage.

If you take the "safe, societal" option that is being suggested to you, it will send you down one path. Most likely, a path that, at some core level, feels wrong. That doesn't feel like you. In fact, it's not you if you compromise what you know at your core and follow the crowd.

If instead you act in alignment with your inner wisdom, things will get better and better. Providence will send all kinds of "miracles" you couldn't have planned or predicted to support your choice. I'm saying this from experience and because hundreds of people have told me their stories about the long-term benefits of trusting their gut and acting in alignment with what was calling them.

Stop Overthinking—Start Doing

"You can't be that kid standing at the top of the waterslide,
overthinking it. You have to go down the chute."

—TINA FEY

Miki Agrawal is a shining example of someone who was brave on be-half of what was calling her. She "went down the waterslide" of faith in-stead of giving in to fears and overthinking it. Miki worked on Wall Street in investment banking in her twenties. She told me, "I had such a tiny apartment I didn't want to spend any time there, so I ate out every night after work. I started having stomach problems because, back then, most restaurant food wasn't very healthy. Turned out I was lactose intolerant and needed to avoid gluten. I went online to research op-tions.

"I discovered pizza accounted for ten percent of all food sales in Manhattan. But pizza's bad for you, right? But what if it wasn't bad for you? I decided to open a farm-to-table restaurant featuring gluten-free pizza."

"Did you have food and beverage experience or a degree in hospitality/ culinary management?"

"Nope, I studied Communications at Cornell and played profes-sional soccer with the New York Magic. So I didn't have industry experi-ence, but I was clear this solved a problem a lot of people had and felt there was a market for it, so I started scouting locations and raising money."

Fast forward, Miki's WILD restaurants have won awards and are going strong nine years after she first opened them. More important, that first entrepreneurial experience led to two additional ventures, an award from *Time* magazine as one of the world's top hundred innova-tors, a seat on the Conscious Capitalism Board (the first millennial), two books (*Do Cool Sh*t* and *Disrupt-Her*) and speaking engagements around the world for such groups as the United Nations and the Transforma-tional Leadership Council.

What's the point? None of this would have happened if Miki hadn't trusted her gut feelings (literally and figuratively) and set her dream in motion even when she wasn't sure it would work.

Stephen Covey is famous for suggesting, "Start with the *end* in mind." But sometimes it's better to start with an *open* mind. Miki couldn't have predicted that the idea in her head would turn her into a wildly successful serial entrepreneur. Her endgame wasn't to become a global thought leader. But that's what's happened. And it happened because she didn't wait until she was certain this would succeed. She bet on herself and trusted she could figure things out on the way.

There's a famous story about Lorne Michaels, longtime director of the TV show *Saturday Night Live*. Comedienne Tina Fey was scrambling to rehearse a last-minute skit and Lorne told her to wrap it up. She said, "But it's not ready." Lorne told her, "*Tina, the show doesn't go on because it's ready, it goes on because it's 11:30.*"

Are you overthinking your dream? Waiting to know *before* you go? Worrying what could go wrong? Instead, why not do your research and then act boldly on your behalf, go down the chute, and trust you can figure things out?

As Kierkegaard pointed out, anxiety is a sign you're confronting the potential of your own development. Do what makes you anxious, not what makes you depressed.

GTS—Google That Stuff—to Determine Next Steps

"Doubts and mistrust are the mere panic of timid imagination, which the steadfast heart will conquer, and the large mind transcend."

—HELEN KELLER

And if you're thinking, "I need more guidance than that. I don't want to just set my dream in motion and have NO idea what I'm doing. That seems risky, even rash."

Got it. Do what Miki did and GTS (Google That Stuff), whatever it is you want to do. Just put into your favorite search engine, "How do you _____?" and put the venture you're considering in the blank.

Want to open your own dog-walking service? Google it and up comes everything you want to know about the costs, insurance, licensing, marketing, and pricing of setting up that business.

Want to take night classes in just about anything? Google it and up comes continuing education classes in your area in everything from how to code to how to be a wedding photographer.

The point is, you don't have to know to go. That's called *perfectionism* which is simply another way to spell *procrastination*. Instead, go online and GTS an industry you want to explore. Attend a meeting. Request their brochure. Register for a webinar. Research next steps.

Whatever you do, don't keep hashing this out in your head. Ideas in your head help no one. Bet on yourself. Be brave on behalf of your vision. Set your venture in motion. As soon as you do, Providence will move too. All kinds of "unforeseen incidents" will arise in your favor. All because you stopped waiting and starting initiating. It's 11:30 . . . time for your show to go on.

In the next chapter, you'll discover how a dolphin helped me understand that "unforeseen incidents" really do arise in our favor when we honor our intuition and the *nudges*.

10

Honor the Nudges, Connect the Dots

"There is a voice that doesn't use words. Listen. . ."

— RUMI

was in Tampa speaking in front of a group of CEOs and needed to be in Savannah a few days later for a conference. I was booked on a train, but when you are on a train, if you see something interesting you want to explore—too bad, you just whiz right by. You don't have the option to stop and investigate it.

My intuition whispered, "Cancel the train. Drive instead."

So, I honored, as Rumi calls it, the "voice that doesn't use words." I set out deliberately not knowing my destination that night. I wanted everything I saw to be new, unexpected.

A few hours in, I decided to GTS what was ahead to see what options I had. Wow, Marineland, the world's first oceanarium and home to the nation's first dolphin encounter was an hour away in St. Augustine. Thank heaven I wasn't on that train and had left room for whims. I called and asked, "Any chance you have an opening in your dolphin encounter this afternoon?"

I lucked out. They did, which is how I found myself swimming with Zach the Dolphin. There were only three of us so our guide turned it into a mini-training session. She whistled Zach over and cued him to turn over on his back so we could stroke his sleek, rubbery sides. She turned to me and said, "Want to give Zach a command?"

Would I like to give Zach a command?!

She said, "Point your finger to the sky." I did. Zach stood on his tail and took off across the pool. Zowee! He swam back and eagerly gulped down his fish reward.

The trainer asked, "Want to give him another command?"

Rhetorical question. "This time, point to the sky and twirl your finger three times."

I pointed my finger to the sky and gave it three big whirls. Zach took off, but this time he dove deep and then rocketed up into the air in a spectacular triple backflip.

I couldn't help myself. It was so unexpected and thrilling, I did a YMCA. I thrust both arms into the sky in a triumphant Y just as the Marineland photographer captured Zach flipping midair, framed between my upstretched arms.

And to think, I hadn't even known Zach existed a few hours before.

Magic Unfolds When We Pay Attention to Our Intuition

"If prayer is you talking to God, intuition is God talking to you."
—WAYNE DYER

When I think back to that experience with Zach, and I think back to it often, I am reminded of the unexpected delights that show up when we pay attention to the nudges.

What do I mean by "nudges"? You know, that "voice that has no words." Those internal inklings we get from time to time to do this, don't do that? What are these nudges?

I had an epiphany about what they might be while watching a TV interview with security consultant and *The Gift of Fear* author Gavin de Becker. The reporter asked what he had learned about fear. De Becker told the reporter he makes it a practice to debrief people who have been kidnapped or assaulted. His first question to them is, *"Did you have any warning?"*

Guess what they all say? "I knew something was wrong." But the vast majority looked around and didn't see "anything wrong" so they dismissed their fears. In other words, they let their intellect overrule their instincts. They thought, "It's broad daylight. I'm in an armored car with bodyguards. What could happen?"

As he described the instincts that alert us when something's about to go *wrong*, I thought, "Doesn't it make sense we also have instincts that alert us when something's about to go *right?*

"If our intuition senses *dissonance*, doesn't it also sense *congruence?*"

Again and again on my travels, my instincts would alert me to congruent opportunities. "Turn here. Take this exit. Stay at this hotel. Talk to that person." Every time I did, it turned out better than I could have imagined. Every time I listened to those internal whispers, even where there was no evidence showing why I should, it led to an aligned opportunity I wouldn't have discovered "on my own."

I still don't know exactly what intuition is. That's a whole other book. What I do know is that our instincts and intuition have our best interests at heart. Those internal nudges have never, not once, steered me *wrong*; they have always steered me *right*.

Have You Left Room in Your Life for Whims?

"The intuitive mind is a sacred gift and the rational mind is a faithful servant. We have created a society that honors the servant and has forgotten the gift."

—ALBERT EINSTEIN

There is a caveat to all this. We have to build in time and space so we have the freedom to follow the nudges when they show up. For years, that was not the case with me. My schedule was so packed that even if I had heard a whisper, I wouldn't have had the option to pursue it. Most of the time, my life was too noisy to notice the whispers, much less honor them.

One of the many wonderful aspects of my Year by the Water was I finally, finally had the time to respond in the moment to nudges. Like that decision to drive instead of take the train. Part of why my gut was resisting that train trip was because whims were not an option. What bliss to have the time for spontaneity, space for serendipity.

Serendipity is defined as "the phenomenon of finding valuable or agreeable things *unintentionally*." Some people feel serendipity is a co-incidence, a happy accident. It's just the opposite. Serendipity is no accident. Intention plays a crucial role in increasing the likelihood of this phenomenon. A coalescing of congruent individuals and events is not happenstance; it is our best future meeting us halfway. Our role is to meet it halfway by staying *alert* to nudges, by *acting* on nudges, and by *appreciating* the good fortune that unfolds when we do.

Serendipity has some requirements though. We need to:

+ Make our intent tangible by writing what we would like to happen in our daily Someday Journal. This crystallizes and communicates our wish.
+ Get quieter. Nudges get drowned out in the noise when we live too loudly.
+ Keep our antenna up for congruent individuals and events that feel right.

- Honor instincts in the moment instead of overruling them with intellect.
- Obey the sixth sense that warns us of dissonance. If something or someone feels "wrong," our instincts are waving a big red flag. Head the other direction.
- Listen to the sixth sense that alerts us to congruence. If something or someone feels "right," connect with it. It is a stepping-stone to serendipity.
- Realize aligned opportunities are fleeting. Act now or lose the chance, maybe forever.
- Know that when a fortuitous coincidence *beats the odds*, it is *no accident*. Providence is working overtime on our behalf. The way to say thank you is to say yes.

Please understand, when we do the above, life gets better and better because we're no longer doing it ourselves. We're cooperating with life instead of controlling it. We're in it together.

Are You Leaving Space for Synchronicity?

"It is always with excitement that I wake up in the morning wondering what my intuition will toss up to me, like gifts from the sea. I work with it and rely on it. It's my partner."

—Jonas Salk

How about you? Is your life so noisy you no longer even notice the nudges? Is your life so jam-packed you don't have the option to follow up on them anyway?

What could you do to change that?

I had an opportunity to speak at NASA Goddard Institute for their Leadership Series and shared some of these ideas in a workshop after my main presentation with a small group of engineers and scientists. One said to me, "Sam, I'm a physicist. Intellectually, I think this is a bunch of hooey. There's no *scientific* evidence proving that what you're saying is true."

He stopped and smiled, "But I have *anecdotal* evidence that it's true. I owe my job to one of those 'happy accidents.' I was out of work for a year. It's hard to find work in my specialty because it's so rare. One night, I got this hunch—out of the blue—to call a college friend I hadn't talked to in years. When he answered his phone and found out it was me, he said, 'I can't believe you called. I was just thinking about you.'

"What are the odds, after years of not having contact, that he would be thinking of me just when I decided to call him? It got better. They had an opening on their project team and needed someone with my background. They flew me out to interview for the job and here I am."

That may sound woo-woo. It's just I've heard too many "out of the blue" stories to dismiss them. I don't know what nudges are, I just know that when we act on them, we facilitate and fast-forward luck.

Honoring Hunches Leads to Luck

"A lot of what we ascribe to luck isn't luck at all.
It's seizing the opportunity and accepting responsibility for your future."
—HOWARD SCHULTZ, FOUNDER OF STARBUCKS

One of my favorite stories about the "luck" that comes our way when we follow our intuition comes from Oliver Uberti. Oliver wanted to work for *National Geographic*. What graphic artist doesn't? He had submitted his résumé but hadn't heard back. Problem was, he would be out of the country during the hiring window for the job he had applied for.

Oliver took his future in his hands. He drove to their Washington, D.C., headquarters, walked up to the security guard's desk, called the Design Director, and told her he was "here for the job."

She had no idea who he was, but was intrigued when she heard about his work and asked him to come in the next day for an interview. He ended up meeting (and befriending) everyone on the team during his three-hour interview, and promised to send dispatches from his travels to Africa.

He left town the next day. While exploring Mozambique and

Swaziland, in one of those fortuitous, beat-the-odds occurrences that seem to happen when we initiate on our own behalf, he found an internet café and was able check his email after being offline for weeks.

There, waiting for him, were several emails from the *National Geographic* Design Director offering him the job, but letting him know she needed to hear from him THAT DAY or she'd have to give the job to the next candidate. Oliver sent back an immediate yes, and ended up being the youngest design editor in the history of the magazine, all because he kick-started his kismet and positioned himself where his luck was most likely to happen.

Oliver's story doesn't stop there. As a result of showing up on the doorstep of his dream, he's now coauthored several award-winning books (including *Where the Animals Go* and *Notes from a Public Typewriter*), delivered talks at Google, the Smithsonian and, the National Storytelling Network, and met and married his soul mate.

As Oliver says, "The rewards for listening to your intuition don't stop after the first one. It's led to all the wonderful things that make my life what it is today."

How about you? When is a time you followed your intuition? How can you show up on the doorstep of your dream and set your luck in motion?

Some people tell me, "You're lucky to live such a charmed life." They're right. I am lucky. I also believe part of the good fortune that has come my way is a result of intentionally putting myself on the doorstep of my dream and acting on congruent "dots" (opportunities) when they show up.

Connect the Dots

"You can't connect the dots looking forward; you can only connect them looking backwards. You have to trust the dots will somehow connect in your future."

— STEVE JOBS

Steve Jobs was brilliant. And I disagree with him on this. I think we *can* connect the dots looking forward as well as backward. And we can do more than *trust* the dots to connect in the future. We can *contribute* dots to create a better future—for ourselves and for others.

Here's what I mean. We're being sent dots all the time. Dots are ideas, opportunities, and individuals. Our role is to pay attention to the ones that *resonate*, collect them, connect them, and act on them. When we do, we set a resonant life in motion that matches our True Priorities.

Remember those connect-the-dots coloring books I referenced in the Introduction of this book? At first, the dots appear to be random. It's up to us to keep drawing connections until they, all of a sudden, come together and make sense. The same thing happens in life. If you get a "random thought," experience a "chance meeting," or get an "out of the blue" urge that calls you, you're supposed to connect with that individual or act on that aligned opportunity. When you do, you set your SerenDestiny (a life where the light is on in your eyes) in motion.

This happened just recently. My friend Inga introduced me to her writing colleague Kristen. Kristen found out I was spending the summer in Boulder and asked if I knew Erin, who runs a training company called Evoso. I didn't, so she introduced us. I emailed Erin, and on impulse, added a sentence asking, "Know anyone who's looking to rent near Wonderland Lake Park?"

Erin got back five minutes later to say a fellow speaker/author had a place right near the lake and was looking for a tenant. What are the odds, right?

I immediately followed up. (Dots have a window of opportunity. They're like fleeting thoughts; we must act on them in the moment.) I connected with her friend Debra and we hit it off. Now I've got a wonderful place to stay, a new friend, and a simpatico colleague.

You can't make this stuff up. You can only honor the hunches when they show up. In particular, the compatible "dot thoughts" that seem to come to us out of the blue. As in, "Add a sentence to the end of your email asking Erin if she has a rental referral."

We're supposed to act on these nudges even if they don't make sense. Especially if they don't make sense. Because "dot thoughts" aren't coming from logic, they're coming from that sixth sense that Gavin de Becker talked about.

When we act on "dot thoughts" that whisper to reach out to this person or say yes to that opportunity, a picture will emerge of a charmed life that is better than anything we could have come up with on our own. Because we didn't do it on our own. We're dancing with life.

So, yes, Steve, we can connect dots looking backward and forward. In fact, it's important to pay back the dots by paying them forward. We can do that by initiating and introducing dots to others. By sending opportunities to people we care about (just like Inga, Kristin, and Erin did for me) to help create a future for them that gets better and better.

Collecting, connecting, and contributing congruent dots creates a rising tide raising all involved. It's a way to do our part and become a part of an enormously satisfying, ever-expanding circle of life.

Think over what has happened in your life the past couple weeks. Has a dot been trying to get your attention? Did you get a nudge to reach out to someone? Did you act on it? Was there an "out of the blue" opportunity that beat the odds? That's a sure sign Providence was working overtime on your behalf.

What Would Happen if You Partnered with Life?

"In baseball and in business, there are three types of baseball players
Those who make it happen, those who watch it happen and those who
wonder what happens."

—TOMMY LASORDA

To riff off what baseball manager Tommy Lasorda said, I believe there are *four* types of people. Those who *make* things happen, those who *watch* what happens, those who *wonder* what happens, and those *who partner with what wants to happen*. We've been taught to plan life. You've probably heard the adage: "Those who fail to plan, plan to fail." What hubris. That's based on the assumption we're the only one involved here.

By all means, start off with a plan, but leave room for serendipitous developments. That's what I did that day I drove up the coast of Florida. But I didn't overplan and lock myself into a predetermined route and timeline. I left that open so I was free to follow up on synchronistic dots that showed up in the moment. Like Marineland and Zach.

> By the way, I got some pushback from a colleague when I told her about swimming with Zach. She said, "Sam, I'm glad that was such a powerful experience for you, but from an animal rights perspective, I don't approve of dolphin encounters."
>
> I thanked her for her feedback and thought long and hard about whether to share that story. I decided to include it for a number of reasons.
>
> First, Marineworld has been an active advocate for marine animal protection for decades and their educational outreach has benefitted thousands of school children.
>
> Secondly, I hope you will see that experience—and the others in this book—as a metaphor. The point of the Zach story was, "What magic might happen if, instead of scheduling every minute of your life, you left room for whims and honored the nudges?" You may never drive into a hurricane, swim with a dolphin or sail the Chesapeake Bay, however I hope those stories motivate you to go with your gut and be a little braver on your behalf because you trust things will work out better when you do. My hope is these stories serve as analogies you can adapt to your circumstances.

Follow What Feels Right

*"We must all make the choice between
what is right and what is easy."*

—J. K. Rowling

A restaurant manager told me, "I don't know what planet you're on, Sam, but some of our employees work two shifts six days a week just to make ends meet. They don't have any spare time to connect dots and follow nudges. Whims aren't on their menu."

I said, "I understand. I'm not saying everyone is in a position to do this. The point is that if you have the option to act on instincts that are aligned with your priorities, it will lead to a life that gets better and better. My friend Myra calls this, 'Living with a compass instead of a map.' She hosted a Someday Salon and contributed this pearl of wisdom during our group discussion."

She said, "In the first half of life, I tried to *make* my life what I wanted it to be. I've relaxed a bit in the second half of life. I understand that not only does everything *not* go according to plan, it's the unplanned things that often bring the greatest gifts. These days I trust my gut to be my guide."

I told her, "I agree. I've 'gentled' the last few years. I believe our life is our lab. My Year by the Water was a lab of what can happen when we *cooperate* with life instead of try to *control* it."

How about you? What's your "connect the dot" story? Everyone I've met has one. A story of a time they got a nudge, trusted it, and magic showed up. A synchronistic encounter that beat the odds and led to something wonderful. How will you keep this top of mind so the next time your instincts alert you to a congruent opportunity and whisper that something's about to go *right*, you answer the call?

11

Put Yourself in Your Own Story

> "If you're searching for that one person
> who will change your life, look in the mirror."
>
> —Roman Price

Whoo-hoo. Today was the day I would be driving California's scenic Pacific Coast Highway from Monterey to Morro Bay.

Due to some unforeseen "dots" that showed up that morning, it was late afternoon before I hit the road. I didn't think much about it until the sun went down and it got dark. And when I say dark, I mean really *dark*. No moon. No light.

If you've taken this spectacular drive, you're familiar with its many hairpin turns. During the day, you can see what's ahead and adapt accordingly. But it was pitch-black and I couldn't see beyond my headlights. I completely lost my equilibrium because I had no idea what was next.

What made it worse was the road had been narrowed to one lane in many places to fix damage caused by recent landslides. The only thing between me and the thousand-foot drop to the ocean below was a rather flimsy-looking guardrail.

A truck zoomed up behind me and flashed its brights. I did what I always did, what I'd been taught to do growing up in a small mountain valley. I looked for the next place I could pull over on the shoulder of the road to let the driver behind me go by.

The only problem? The shoulder was gravel. And shorter than anticipated. The harder I braked, the more I slid. My car finally came to a stop a few feet from the cliff's edge.

I sat there and shook. The truck was long gone. It was just me, the road, and (and I know this sounds dramatic but it was what I was thinking) the realization that my habit of putting others first had just about cost me my life.

Does any of this sound familiar? Do you put other people first, yourself last?? Is your go-to response, "No, you go ahead."

If you're a parent, caregiver, entrepreneur, or executive, this may have become your norm. Yet serving others at the cost of ourselves can become an extreme . . . and any extreme is unhealthy.

Self-sacrifice comes at a price. We lose our equilibrium and can end up compromising our health and happiness. What's worse, when we habitually take ourselves out of our own story, we teach the people around us we don't count, that what we want and need doesn't matter. Is that what we want to teach? Is martyrdom the model we want to pass along?

The Consequences of *Always* Putting Others First

"In influencing others, example is not the main thing;
it's the only thing."

— ALBERT SCHWEITZER

That close call motivated me to evaluate my lifelong default of putting other people's needs before my own. *Where* did I learn to do this? *Why* did I learn to do this?

Well, as with many things, it started at home. My mom was an example of unconditional love. She was also sick the last twenty years of her life, dealing with the effects of multiple sclerosis (which was later discovered to have been a misdiagnosed, slow-growing brain tumor).

My mom was in pain almost every day. If I put my hand anywhere near her neck, I could feel the pain waves vibrating off it. Yet she didn't want to be "a burden" so she soldiered on. I would ask, "Can I help with dinner, Mom? Want me to do the dishes?"

"No, thanks, hon. I've got it."

She wanted my sister, brother, and me to have a good life and didn't want to be a "downer," so she rarely, if ever, talked about her illness. She always wanted to know what *we* were doing, what was going on at school and with our friends. She never asked for anything herself, and if we offered, she usually demurred, not wanting to "put us out."

My mom did what she thought was the right thing, at great personal cost. What we learned from her example though was probably not what she intended.

Yes, we received and learned about unconditional love, and I will always be grateful for that.

We also learned to not ask for help or accept help. We learned to be "strong" and not share our pain. We learned that the last thing you wanted was to be a "burden." We learned that putting others first, and not thinking of our pain or needs, was the noble thing, the right thing, to do.

Serving others *is* a noble thing. There are hundreds of quotes claiming that the meaning of life is to be found in service. For example, Rabindranath Tagore wrote, "I slept and dreamt that life was joy. I awoke and saw that life was service. I acted and behold, service was joy."

Yet sometimes service is not joy. Sometimes, service becomes unhealthy people-pleasing.

A college counselor told me, "Sam, I don't have kids but I do have students. Many are away from home for the first time. They're lonely, confused, and overwhelmed. My heart goes out to them. I've given some my home phone number so they can call if they're having a tough time. Good idea in theory, not so good in practice. I spend many evenings on the phone mitigating one crisis after another. My husband is starting to resent this and I can't blame him. Plus, I'm getting burned out because I never get a chance to recharge."

I told her, "Good for you for being there for your students. The question is, are you also being there for yourself? Think about the Law of Unintended Consequences. What we accept, we teach. What are you teaching by ignoring your health and husband, and by not having any boundaries around your time and access?"

"But I feel so sorry for these kids. They all have a story."

"I get it, but you're thinking only of their story, not your own. Where are you in your own story?"

"But I can't just cut them off and turn my back on them."

"I'm not suggesting you turn your back on them. I'm suggesting you not turn your back on yourself. I'm suggesting you set up some boundaries so you can serve others *and* yourself. Instead of being available to your students every single night, what is a fairer balance?"

Suffice it to say, she created a written policy explaining her "evening office hours" that she posted and handed to students. They still have an option to contact her in case of an emergency; otherwise there's a process for scheduling time with her on campus during the day.

She contacted me later to say our conversation, and her new policy, taught her a valuable lesson. "I never realized how much I was devaluing myself by focusing exclusively on my students' needs. My husband thanks you, I thank you. Someday, my students may even thank you for having someone model that it's not selfish to put yourself in your own story."

How about you? Are you running on empty? Burnout is a clear sign you're not enforcing your boundaries—or you don't have any boundaries. It's a clear sign you are putting others first—and yourself last.

Next time you're about to compromise your well-being with "No, you go ahead. You go first"—*Stop!* Remind yourself that you matter. What you want and need counts. You can serve others *and* yourself. It's not either/or. Put yourself back in your own story. It's not selfish. It's smart.

What We Accept, We Teach

"If your compassion does not include yourself, it is incomplete."

—JACK KORNFIELD

I was talking about this issue of sacrificing ourselves in the name of service with Gail Sheehy, the author of *Passages*. She told me that one of the most startling research findings for her work on millennials is that "more than 50 percent of young people under the age of thirty don't want children any time soon because *they saw their parents sacrifice themselves for their kids and they're not ready to do the same.*"

Yikes. Is that what we parents intended? In our eagerness to raise happy kids, did we set an unhealthy example? What were we modeling when we set our own hobbies aside and attended every soccer game, dance recital, and martial-arts match? What did we teach when, as adults, we abandoned our own dreams and took ourselves out of the story? The question is, what can we do to create a better balance?

One way is to picture "The Serve Others–Serve Ourselves Continuum." It's easier to get a clearer understanding of whether we're being *selfless* or *selfish* if we make this vague concept visually concrete. Picture a continuum line with Serve Others on the left end and Serve Ourselves on the right end.

If you're exhausted and it seems you don't have any energy for your needs, ask yourself, "Where am I right now on the selfless-selfish continuum? Think of the activities you do each week. How many serve others? How many serve you? If the continuum is heavily weighted to the left, it's not selfish to carve out some time to do *something* for yourself —whether that's getting a massage or swapping kid duties with your spouse so you can sleep in one morning.

Serve Others Only _____ Serve Ourselves Only

That college counselor was originally way over on the left because she was only thinking of her students' needs. Her goal was to get closer to the middle of the continuum and spend more time attending to her own needs instead of neglecting them.

If you have been turning your back on your own needs, remember what we talked about in chapter 5. Put a date on the calendar and correct this imbalance now instead of promising you'll put yourself in your story *someday*. What True Priority of yours is getting ignored? Schedule it. Do it. Remember, taking responsibility for your well-being isn't selfish, it's inspiring.

Is It Time to Be the Lead in Your Own Life?

"The stories we tell ourselves are what make our
dreams come true."

— SHERI SALATA

I had the unique pleasure of interviewing Sheri Salata. You may know her as the Executive Producer of Oprah Winfrey's TV show and Co-President of Harpo Studios and OWN Network. What you may not know is that after twenty years of facilitating other people's stories (often from six thirty in the morning to eleven thirty at night seven days a week), she decided it was time to take the lead in her own story. And what does she call her new media company, founded with longtime friend Nancy Hala? Story.co.

Be sure to check out their uplifting podcast series "This Is Fifty with Sheri & Nancy" and "The Pillar Life," where they help people take the lead in their own life and tell a new story.

When I asked Sheri what motivated her to make this career switch, she said, "I thought, 'If not now, when?' I was ready to adapt a new regimen of radical self-care, and I was really inspired by all the entrepreneurs we featured at OWN. I saw them making their dreams come true and decided I wanted to sing my own song while I still could. I saw some people who dropped the ceiling on their dreams because they were afraid of not getting what they want. I want people to know that the

story they tell themselves is the most important story they're going to
tell. It will determine what they look like, feel like, and what kind of
ride they will have for the rest of their life."

How about you? What story have you been telling yourself? Have
you been facilitating other people's stories and not your own? Is it time
to tell a new story? As Sheri points out, "Your story isn't over, it's just
starting. All you need to do is take the lead."

Doing What You Like Isn't Indulgent; It's an Investment

"It's not your job to like me; it's mine."

— BYRON KATIE

From now on, keep your antenna up for when you're taking yourself out
of your story. It's not always dramatic, it can be a drip-drip-drip effect
over time that results in a "near-life experience." We get so accustomed
to giving up what we want, we no longer even ask for it.

For example, I was on a budget while traveling, so usually opted to
stay in, shall we say, *economy* properties instead of the more *expensive*
waterfront properties.

I had a consult near LAX, the Los Angeles airport, so I went online to book a hotel. Wait a minute. What was this? A hotel on the water
in Marina del Rey, only ten minutes from the airport? And discounted
so it was only ten dollars more than the cookie-cutter Century Boule-
vard box hotels? Sold!

What a joy it was checking-in at the tropical Jamaican Inn that
looked as if it was transplanted from the Bahamas.

The front desk clerk asked, "Where you from?" I told him about
my Year by the Water. He was so intrigued that he spontaneously upgraded me on the spot. I walked into my spacious waterfront suite
and was met with a stunning sunset framed by towering palm trees. I
opened the sliding-glass doors, walked out onto the balcony, threw
my head back, breathed in the salt air, and marveled at a pair of peli-
cans doing majestic fly-bys.

My friend Glenna called in the middle of my reverie and revelry. She heard the happiness in my voice and asked, "What's going on?"

I told her how happy it made me to be on the water. She was puzzled, "Sam, you're on your Year by the Water. Don't you normally stay on the water?"

I explained about my need to be frugal and that I was more often at the back of the property She paused and then said, "Sam, wouldn't you rather spend six months overlooking the water than twelve months overlooking the parking lot?"

Yes, I would, Glenna. Yes, I would.

Are You Settling for Parking Lots When What You Want Is Water?

"Cats seem to go on the principle that it never does any harm to ask for what you want."

—JOSEPH WOOD KRUTCH

How about you? Have you been frugal (financially *and* emotionally) for so long you no longer even ask for what you want? Are you constantly compromising—settling for rooms overlooking the freeway when it's waterfront views you crave?

I understand the importance of being fiscally and psychologically responsible. There are times when a budget mentality is necessary. And there are also times when doing something that lights us up is the gift that keeps on giving. For me, waking up to water, writing by the water, and going for an energizing walk along water sets up a happiness ripple effect. It makes my head, heart, and soul sing . . . for days.

I could have been in a dingy room overlooking the garage or in one of those hermetically sealed high-rise hotels that suck the soul right out of you. Instead, *here* I was, being inspired by *where* I was. The spirit-lifting view of people outdoors in nature kayaking, paddle-boarding, running, and enjoying their life made my soul sing.

Life isn't supposed to be a drudge. We are supposed to be glad we're alive. Please understand that doing something each week that makes your soul sing isn't indulgent, it's an investment in a more energized life.

I am not suggesting we can or should put ourselves first *all* the time. It's important to continue to take care of others and live within our means. Yet an authentic life is one in which we put ourselves in our own story . . . without apology or guilt. What does that look like for you?

In our next chapter, you'll discover ways to climb out of ruts and replace habits that might be getting in the way of your happiness.

12

Beware of the Rubber Band of Routine Snapping Back

"It seems as if the second half of man's life is made up of nothing but the habits he accumulated during the first half."

—FYODOR DOSTOYEVSKY

Full confession. I've shared stories of sailing the Chesapeake Bay, swimming with Zach the Dolphin, and staying in Marina del Ray. But the truth? There *wasn't* a lot of water in the first three months of my Year by the Water.

What happened? It wasn't just being on a budget. The truth is, the rubber band of routine snapped back. Here's what I mean.

I was on the phone with my business manager, Cheri. We were discussing several potential speaking engagements and she said, "Sam, are you sure you want to say yes to these?"

"What do you mean?"

"Well, I reviewed your calendar. You've spent sixty of the last ninety days in cities, business hotels, and office buildings nowhere near the water. Is that what you wanted?"

Arrggh. No, that's not what I wanted. Why had I reverted to my habit of filling my calendar with business commitments?

Cheri had a theory about this. "Remember the day you left for your trip and I asked, 'What do you want *most* for your trip?' Remember what you said? You said, 'I know what I *don't* want. For this to turn into business as usual . . . just on the road.'"

As soon as she said it, I *did* remember it. I expressed what I *didn't* want. And, as previously discussed, when we focus on what we don't want, that's what we're going to get.

In my defense, there were good reasons that burst out of my mouth. The weeks leading up to my departure had been intense with downsizing, house cleaning, and good-byes. Still. I'm supposed to know better. I had told myself, "I *don't* want this to be business as usual," so that's what I got. The question is, if I *knew* this was counterproductive, why did I *do* this?

We Get What We Focus On

"I want to live my life so that my nights are not filled with regrets."
— D. H. Lawrence

I asked Cheri why she thought I reverted to filling my calendar again, when my Year by the Water was supposed to be about NOT going 24/7.

She said, "Sam, think about it. You've been a single mom and entrepreneur for years. To you, a full calendar meant success and security. It meant you could breathe easy because you could pay bills. When you set off on your Year by the Water, for the first time in a long time, you had 'empty' days on your calendar. I think that was, at some level, cause for panic."

She was right. My income is entirely derived from client work. No clients = no money. So, for the last three decades, empty days on my calendar meant I needed to get busy on biz dev.

But if I'm honest about it, and I want to be honest about it, *ego* probably played a role in why I kept saying yes to clients. It's gratifying to have people value what I do. It felt good to be "in demand." As a consultant, having people want to work with me was proof of my worth.

However, one of the purposes of this trip was to be creatively adventurous. I was supposed to be doing the "opposite of my always" instead of sliding right back into old routines.

I wanted to "abdicate" this long-held association that a full calendar equaled success. I no longer wanted to equate being "booked solid" with being secure, valued, and worthy.

Cheri said, "You had clarity around a similar issue several years ago. Remember?"

As soon as she said this, I knew exactly what she was talking about. The week Andrew left for Virginia Tech (Tom was already there), I was walking my dog around the lake when I ran into a neighbor. When she discovered both my sons were at college, she said, "You're rattling around in that big house all by yourself? You must be suffering from *empty-nest* syndrome."

The thought had never occurred to me. I smiled and said, "I don't have an *empty nest*, I have an *open nest*."

Her eyes flew open. "A what?!"

"An *open* nest. Empty means no one's there. I'm there. My sons aren't gone from my life. They're happy, healthy, and doing exactly what they're supposed to be doing at this stage of their life. We're still connected and we're all free to come and go from this open nest whenever we please."

"Wow. I never thought of it that way."

That "open nest" reframe provided a more positive, proactive perspective. I didn't have *empty* days; I had *open* days. Instead of seeing them as *un-booked* days, I saw them as *unplanned* days, when I had the freedom to respond in the moment to whatever whims caught my fancy.

As mentioned before, one of the many things I appreciate about Cheri is how practical and proactive she is. She said, "Okay, to make sure you don't give in to the pressure to say yes to every business opportunity that comes your way, let's put some boundaries in place. How will you hold yourself accountable for not reverting to your old habit of filling your calendar?"

Good question. Here's how.

How Will You Hold Yourself Accountable for New Behaviors?

"If your boundaries don't have numbers in them, they're not boundaries."

—SAM HORN

When it comes to changing habits, I've got one word for you. *Metrics.* If we don't ground new behaviors and boundaries in metrics, they'll be too vague. Intentions aren't enforceable unless we assign specific, tangible numbers to them.

Cheri and I allocated a certain number of days each month for "client work," and a certain number of days each month for "water work." I still had financial obligations, still wanted and needed to make money and work with clients, I just didn't want to do it seven days a week.

As soon as we assigned numbers to my boundaries, they were no longer wishy-washy. I knew exactly when I had maxed out on business commitments for the month. It gave me the clarity (and courage) to schedule them for another month, to refer them to a colleague, or to say "No, thank you."

Have You Reverted to Old Habits?

"It takes guts to get out of ruts."

—ROBERT H. SCHULLER

How about you? Despite promising to take time "off" for a Today, Not Someday priority, are you continuing to fill your calendar with work commitments? Has the Rubber Band of Routine snapped back and you've reverted to a default of going 24/7?

If so, look at your language. Are you focusing on what you *don't* want? Are you telling yourself, "I *don't* want to work weekends." If so, change your words. Start expressing what you will do instead of what you won't. "Weekends are family time."

Second, assign metrics to your intentions so the rubber band of routine doesn't snap back as it did for this startup founder. He told me, "The first few years were all-consuming. I pretty much worked around the clock. I missed a lot of my kids' activities and I regret it. I recently sold my company and promised my family I'd take a year off before starting another business. My sons are both into travel soccer, so I volunteered to be 'team dad.' I thought it'd be a good way to spend time with them." He laughed ruefully, "It hasn't quite turned out that way."

"How so?"

"If you've ever been around kids' competitive sports—whether it's soccer, softball, or swimming . . . you know it can become all-consuming. I thought I'd be passing out oranges, coordinating travel, maybe doing some fund-raising for uniforms. That was naïve. I spend almost every night on the phone with parents complaining the coach is playing favorites or their kid isn't getting enough playing time. The league asked me to be on the board and I agreed. I had no idea what I was getting into. They told me there were only two meetings a month during season, but they didn't mention the back-and-forth emails about eligibility disputes, umpire complaints, and weather reschedules. I'm not spending any time with my sons . . . *again.*"

"So, what are you going to do about it?"

"I'm not sure. I made commitments to the league and team. I can't back out now."

"Hmmm. Want some questions you can ask yourself to see if there might be ways to bring your Time Priorities and True Priorities back into balance?"

"Is that a rhetorical question?"

Clarity Questions to Help Us Stay True to Our True Priorities

"I'm not telling you it will be easy. I'm telling you it will be worth it."
— ART WILLIAMS

1. What is a new behavior I want to do? A True Priority I want to spend more time on? What percentage of my time am I spending on it now?

2. What percentage of my time am I spending on my other responsibilities? Is there an end date for these responsibilities? Are they temporary or seasonal? Will they be over soon or are they "permanent and perpetual"?

3. Fast-forward to the end of this year. Will you be glad or sad you focused on these other responsibilities? Will you regret you neglected a True Priority project and wish you could have a do-over? How will you feel about this in five years?

4. Are you honoring these other responsibilities because you "have to," "want to," said you would, or because you think you should? At what cost? At *whose* cost?

5. Who and what really matters to you now—and in the long run? Are you honoring them with your time or have you allowed yourself to get pulled off track?

6. Can you get creative and delegate or renegotiate your responsibilities—or reduce some of the time spent on them—so you're freed up to focus on a True Priority?

7. Can you establish a boundary with metrics around a True Priority so you honor it instead of continuing to serve others and not yourself? What is that boundary?

Get Clear About What Will Matter in the Long Run

"The light at the end of the tunnel is not an illusion. The tunnel is."
— COFFEE MUG SLOGAN

That startup founder got back in touch weeks later to say that talking through those questions had given him clarity about what had been a "muddy" situation up until then.

He said, "I gave the Board Chair my one month 'notice' and told him I'd find a replacement. I asked another parent to share Team Dad responsibilities so I'm not shouldering those all on my own. We instituted a policy that parent requests will be handled at games, practices, and between seven and eight on weeknights. We don't text, email, or pick up the phone at other times. That's family time. At first, I thought we'd get push-back from parents. And it's true, a few were upset that we weren't available 24/7. But the rest understand what we're doing and are supporting it."

That's the point of asking yourself those Clarity Questions. You may feel you're locked into current responsibilities and think there are no options. When it comes to honoring a True Priority, there are *always* options.

Remember Harry Chapin's evocative song "Cat's in the Cradle?" His son wants to play, but the dad has planes to catch, bills to pay. His son wants to know when he is coming home and the father puts him off until later.

Later, when the father is finally ready to spend time with his son, he calls only to discover his son is too busy for him. The father laments, too late, that his son had grown up to be just like him.

Are you in a "Cat's in a Cradle" situation where you are assuming the people you want to spend time with will want to spend time with you? Are you assuming that a True Priority will be there waiting when you're ready for it?

That is a preventable path to regrets. Pick up the phone right now and call someone you've been meaning to get in touch with. Allocate a time boundary around a True Priority to prevent yourself from sliding back into busy ruts. Do it now, not later. Later may be too late.

How Will You Keep the Rubber Band of Routine from Snapping Back?

"Some people believe holding on and hanging in are signs of strength. However, there are times it takes more strength to know when to let go and then to do it."

—ANN LANDERS

I was talking with my friend Lee (the one who runs forums for executives and traveled with me to the James Taylor concert) about boundaries. She said, "I needed to hear this today."

"What's been happening?" I asked.

"I was running on empty and wondering why. I looked at my calendar and realized I had been out every night for twelve nights straight. And I'm an introvert! It's just that these were all worthy causes. I just couldn't say no."

I told her, "Lee, you're such a public person, it's crucial to have objective (vs. subjective) boundaries around how many events you'll attend every week. It's crazy-making to make case-by-case decisions, because then you see the tree and not the forest. You think, 'I've got to support their fund-raiser; they supported mine,' or 'I can't say no to him, he's on my board.' You end up saying yes to everyone and no to yourself."

"Sam, that sounds good in theory, but I'm not sure how to do it in practice. Surely there are exceptions to this?"

I told her, "Exceptions are the slippery slope of boundaries. I learned this the hard way at the Maui Writers Conference at the Grand Wailea Resort. We had an incredible Friday night program featuring humorist Dave Barry followed by Hawaiian singing sensation Keali'i Reichel, who was bringing his entire halau (hula dance group) fresh from a performance at Carnegie Hall.

"Our ballroom was sold out and we were turning people away. A board member from the Big Island cornered me during the reception, distraught. He had called our MWC office the week before to buy tickets. A staff member had told him there was no need, he could just get them at the door. He flew his entire family over to Maui, only to be told 'Sorry, no tickets available.'

"All I could think about was how supportive he'd been over the years, and it was important to return the favor by making room for him and his family. So, I told him I'd get him in.

"Big mistake. That decision made sense to me under the circumstances, but it backfired big time. Several people overheard what I'd done and got really upset (understandably so). My exception to the rule had opened Pandora's box. I created a mess by thinking of this one person instead of seeing the situation in context."

Lee said, "Got it. I don't want to open Pandora's box and I don't want to keep making exceptions to my rule. I'm setting a max of four nights out a week. And I'll enforce it by remembering how vital it is to my well-being to recharge at home the other three nights."

How about you? What are your time boundaries for your True Priorities And if you're tempted to make exceptions to your rule, just ask yourself if you really want to open Pandora's box.

CELEBRATE What's Right with Life, Right Here, Right Now

"I've always had the feeling that life loves the liver of it."
—MAYA ANGELOU

EVALUATE

RELOCATE   GENERATE

INNOVATE   ABDICATE

NEGOTIATE   INITIATE

INTEGRATE   **CELEBRATE**

AFFILIATE

ife Hack 5 shares a variety of ways to enjoy your life right here, right now—even in the midst of trying circumstances. You'll discover that while there may be stressful situations in your life beyond your control, there are little things you can do on a daily basis to make life worth living.

13

Live in Day-Right Compartments

"Live in day-tight compartments."

—DALE CARNEGIE

Thanks to my friend Mary for introducing a pivotal way to live in day-*tight*, day-*right* compartments. We were in Corona del Mar for our annual mastermind retreat. What's a mastermind? A group of people who meet on a regular basis, in person or virtually, to brainstorm priority goals and hold each other accountable for achieving and celebrating them.

Mary had dated a colonel years ago who was assigned to the Air Force Academy. She admired the long-term bonds he had maintained with classmates for decades. She proposed we form the same type of "We'll be there for each other—no matter what" relationship where we had each other's back and front. We agreed to quarterly calls and annual weekend retreats where we do a review-preview of our personal and professional lives, identify a Today, Not Someday dream, and strategize how we can make it a reality and contribute to each other's success.

It was Mary's turn to be in charge. We settled into our chairs, got out our notebooks, and looked at her with anticipation. With a Mona Lisa smile she asked, "What's your morning practice?"

We gave her a puzzled Scooby-Doo look. "Our what?!"

"You know, your morning practice. Do you meditate? Write in a gratitude journal? What?"

Denise and I shrugged and said we didn't have one.

"Hmmm. It's time to get one. The first few minutes of each day are often the only part of that day we can control. And how we start our day sets the tone for our day. If we're shocked awake by an alarm, we're already in a state of fight or flight. If we check email or watch the news, we're already overwhelmed by our to-do's and all the bad news."

"So, what should we do instead?"

"Establish a morning practice that feels good. First thing I do is fix my favorite tea, sit in my chair by the window, and write in my gratitude journal. For those twenty minutes, everything's right with my world." She paused. "Sometimes, that's the only part of the day that feels that way."

Mary was right. Following that retreat, I initiated a daily morning practice and discovered it is a way to live in "day-right compartments." As Mary pointed out, I can't control what happens the rest of the day; I can control what I do those first few minutes. I've found that spending ten minutes doing my "goals and gratefuls" is the lead domino of a good day. When I invest that time, everything else falls in line.

Get Your Day Off to a Good Start with Your Someday Journal

"Action is the antidote to despair."

—JOAN BAEZ

How about you? Do you have a morning practice? What is it? How does it impact you?

A friend, who was sued by a former employee, was devastated that this individual (who she had invested a lot of time in) had turned on her.

She was both angry and depressed (it's said depression is suppressed rage) as legal bills mounted up and she was forced to spend hours tracking down communications from months ago to prove the suit was unfounded.

I asked, "Are you journaling?"

"Who has time?!"

I told her, "It's easy to 'get in our head' when dealing with hard times. A proactive way to deal with challenges is to 'journal them out.' It's a tangible way to get what's bothering us off our chest and onto paper so it's not swirling around in our head and clogging up our emotional operating system."

I'm not the only proponent of the positive impact of journaling. Yale, Stanford, and Harvard have all published research that shows gratitude journals can "improve the immune system, reduce illness, anxiety, and depression and strengthen relationships."

Your Someday Journal is a tangible tool for choosing what you're going to dwell on that day. My friend certainly didn't choose to be sued, and she couldn't choose what thoughts came into her head. She could choose how long they stayed there.

Mark Twain said, "Drag your thoughts away from your troubles—by the ears, by the heels, or any other way, so you can manage it; it's the healthiest thing a body can do."

The Someday Journal is not just a way to drag your thoughts away from your troubles. It's a way to track progress on a True Priority and center yourself in how you want to show up that day. And, it features inspiring quotes so you'll have something to look forward to every day.

My hope is this journal is a joy, not a chore. I experimented with different styles and asked people which they preferred. Many said they liked variety instead of the same predictable format, so each day is different and features something new. Here's a sample page.

SOMEDAY Is Not a Day in the Week Journal
QUOTE FOR TODAY:

"I'm always persistently outside my comfort zone."
—TORY BURCH

What does this quote mean to me? How will I act on it and integrate it into my life today? _____

_____

CELEBRATE: What will I do to put the light on in my eyes today, even if it's for a few moments?

INITIATE: What is one specific thing I'll do today to make tangible progress on a True Priority? _____

_____

EVALUATE: What is the best thing that happened to me today?

_____

_____

_____

How about you? Do you journal? How has it impacted your life? Natalie Goldberg says, journaling is "having a relationship with your mind." The moments we journal are often the only uninterrupted moments we have all day to focus on a True Priority. It's a way to keep what we care about top of mind instead of letting it slide out-of-sight, out-of-mind. It's worth it.

Why Journaling Is Like Going to the Gym

"How we spend our days is, of course, how we spend our lives."
— ANNIE DILLARD

A salon attendee asked, "Does your journal have a way to review the day? I like jotting down something that went well before going to bed because it helps me have sweet dreams."

I told her, "I agree. Starting and ending our day on a positive note bookends our day and gives it a satisfying full-circle sense of completion and closure."

Another woman said, "I am not a morning person. I usually hit the snooze button several times before dragging myself out of bed. So, journaling first thing in the morning was not on my list of priorities. Then, I saw an article in *Wall Street Journal* about 'rude-colored glasses.'"

"What's that?"

"It was based on research from University of Maryland which found that if we witness rudeness in the morning, we tend to see more instances of it throughout the day and we are more likely to be rude ourselves. I decided I didn't want to start my day as a grump anymore. I told myself I'd journal every morning for a month, and if at the end of a month I wanted to ditch it, I would."

"So, what happened?"

She smiled and said, "After a month, I decided that journaling is like going to the gym. I don't always want to do it, but I'm always glad I did it. I like looking back through it and being reminded of how far I've come. It keeps me on track."

What Can You Do to Contribute to Your Well-Being—Today and Every Day?

"Each morning we are born again.
What we do today is what matters most."

— BUDDHA

In addition to journaling, there's another way to live in day-right compartments. This is especially helpful if you're going through a tough time.

I had an opportunity to coach the speakers at TEDx South Lake Tahoe including Golbie Kamarei, who introduced meditation to a Wall Street financial institution that manages trillions of dollars. She said, "The ambition in this industry is off the charts, and so is the stress. An executive told me his two-year-old son didn't recognize him when he returned home from an overseas trip. I thought we needed something to counteract this nonstop pressure so I offered a meditation class. Imagine my surprise when sixty 'suits' showed up for our first class. Word got out and now BlackRock has meditation offerings in sixty locations worldwide."

I asked, "What's the most important benefit of meditation for people who are crazy-busy?"

Golbie said, "We tracked results and compiled statistics that show it improves job performance, productivity, and peace of mind. But for me, what's even more important is that stressed-out people tell me they've stopped trading off their internal well-being for external success. Their mantra has become, 'What can I do to take care of myself *today?*'"

I can attest to the benefits of meditation. Several years ago, in the midst of my "busy season," a friend gave me a gift certificate to a spa. When I walked in, the masseuse took one look at me and said, "I can tell you're not breathing. People hold their breath when they're tense because they feel like they're underwater. But breathing shallowly means you live life on the surface."

Gee whiz. A massage therapist with the emphasis on *therapist*. "What else?" I asked.

"When we don't breathe, we don't air out emotions or release toxins inside us. As a result, they accumulate in our body and poison our mind and system. I'll give you a massage, but you would do yourself a favor by learning how to belly-breathe."

"What's that?"

"Our breathing usually *reflects* our mental state. The goal of belly-breathing is to *direct* our mental state. By breathing slowly and deeply, we can actually slow a racing heart and mind and counteract stress. Next time you're under pressure, try this. You don't have to sit in a lotus position or go to a yoga class. You can do it anytime, anywhere . . . even at work while sitting at your desk."

Five-Minute Belly-Breathing Meditation

"Meditation is the ultimate rest. It keeps life fresh."

— HUGH JACKMAN

Feeling stressed? Try this.

1. Sit tall. Relax your shoulders and arms. Rest your hands on your thighs.
2. Inhale from the bottom up. Your lungs have three parts: a lower space in your abdomen, a middle space above your navel, and an upper space in your chest. As you breathe in through your nose, fill the lower space first. Then fill your middle space with energy and air. Finally feel your chest and upper back open up as air enters the area.
3. It can help to place your palm on your abdomen, so you can feel it expanding and contracting with each breath. Many of us have been taught to suck in our gut. That may be appropriate for other times, not for now. Go ahead and relax those tight muscles. The goal is to feel your waistline going in and out, not maintaining a flat stomach.
4. When your lungs feel comfortably full (don't force it), stop, then

exhale your air in a smooth, continuous movement (not a
whoosh!) with the air streaming out of your mouth.
5. The can be done over a beat of six counts *in* and a beat of six
counts (or seconds) *out*. You might want to mentally count "One,
two, three, four, five, six" when you inhale, and mentally count
"One, two, three, four, five, six" when you exhale.

I will always be grateful to my friend for gifting me with that spa certificate, and to that massage therapist for her Yoda-like advice on how
to center myself anytime, anywhere. She was right. If I'm feeling uptight,
I'm usually not breathing. It's amazing how I can calm myself and tap
back into that core of happiness in just about any situation if I belly-
breathe.

How about you? Are you under a lot of pressure? Dealing with challenging circumstances? Do you meditate? Belly-breathe? If so, what
impact has it had on your ability to counteract stress? If not, try it. It's
free, you can do it in five minutes anytime, anywhere . . . and it works.

How to Create Tranquility

"When we are unable to find tranquility within ourselves,
it is useless to seek it elsewhere."
— LA ROCHEFOUCAULD

Want your belly-breathing to be even more beneficial? Instead of mentally counting *numbers*, select six *emotions* you would like to feel or six
characteristics you would like to embody. It helps if your words are one
syllable so they're simple to say.

Repeating a mantra as you inhale and exhale serves as an affirma-
tion. Not only are you belly-breathing, which has all kinds of health benefits, you are imprinting how you want to show up in the world, which
has all kinds of psychological benefits.

Here are the words I use when belly-breathing. And, by the way, this
isn't just an ideal way to start the day. And it's not just for counteract-

ing stress. When I go to bed, all I have to do is belly-breathe with my six mantra's "B-e-e-e-e...S-e-e-e-e" ... "H-e-a-l-t-h" ... "W-e-a-l-t-h" ... and the next thing I know ... it's morning.

Breath 1. *Be ... See.*

Breath 2. *Health ... Wealth.*

Breath 3. *Listen ... Love.*

Breath 4. *Now ... Wow.*

Breath 5. *Flow ... Let it go.*

Breath 6. *Receive ... Breathe.*

My colleague, Adam Markel, author of the business bestseller *Pivot*, repeats the mantra "I love my life, I love my life" every morning when he wakes up. He told me, "If something's not going well in my life, it's amazing the power those four words have to put me in a good mood."

How about you? How will you start your day to set the tone for the day? What will you do to de-stress? How will you breathe in and breathe out how you want to show up?

Jack Kornfield said, "When we get too caught up in the busyness of the world, we lose connection with one another - and ourselves." What will you do, today, to counteract the busyness of the world and live in day-right compartments? And if you'd like more ways to stay connected with who and what matters, keep reading.

14

Get Out of Your Head and Come to Your Senses

"The moment one gives close attention to anything, even a blade of grass, it becomes a mysterious, awesome, indescribably magnificent world in itself."

— HENRY MILLER

know it's a cliché, but have you ever seen anything so beautiful it took your breath away?

My friend and former *National Geographic* photographer Dewitt Jones found out about my Year by the Water and invited me to a private photography workshop at Monet's garden in France.

It took me about one second to say yes to this extraordinary opportunity to experience Monet's fabled lily pond early in the morning before the gardens were opened to the public.

We started with a fresh croissant and French-pressed coffee and then walked down the quaint streets of Giverny to meet the head gardener at the green door. Yes, those were the directions.

Precisely at 7:00 a.m., he opened the doors and ushered our small group into a little piece of heaven on earth. The others started oohing and aahing at the rows of irises, roses, peonies, and every type of flower imaginable. Me? Well, I had a date with a lily pond.

Dewitt led me through a tunnel to the secluded gardens on the other side of the road. We followed a stream path through a dense bamboo forest, rounded a corner, and there was the famous green arched bridge framed by weeping willows. My eyes feasted on palettes of pink, lilac, and fuchsia—a living, breathing testimony to nature's abundance. This was the opposite of a perfectly manicured garden with tightly clipped hedges and rigidly controlled design.

This was, as Dewitt put it, a *profusion*. I was intrigued with his just-right word and looked it up later. Profusion is defined as a "lavish display, extravagant." That's exactly what was spread out all around us. Ralph Waldo Emerson said, "The earth laughs in flowers." I found myself laughing out loud, not because anything was funny, but because I was filled with sheer joy at what I was seeing. I felt pulled along the garden paths, drinking it all in, filled with a timeless sense of wonder. The trees were teeming with the coos and calls of birds greeting the new day. It was alive. I was alive. I was immeasurably grateful for both.

Why was this so important? Because many people think they'll be happy *when, after, as soon as, someday*. They'll be happy *when* they retire. *After* they get a raise. *As soon as* they lose those ten pounds. *Someday* when they find the love of their life.

Please understand, if we're not happy *here*, we won't be happy *there*.

Yes, it's important to have a purposeful goal or meaningful dream we're working toward . . . but your happiness can't be dependent on achieving that. Because that would mean your happiness is always *out there* somewhere, and you want your happiness to be *right here*.

The way to have happiness here and now is to see things as if for the first or last time, and to use your senses to imprint and truly appreciate the blessing of being alive.

Do You Have Juice in Your Camera?

"If the only prayer we ever said was 'Thank you,'
that would be enough."

— MEISTER ECKHART

An accountant named Frank pushed back, "Sam, I pretty much wake up, go to the office, have lunch at my desk, and drive home. If I do get out on weekends, it's to run errands, get groceries, see a movie, or eat at a restaurant. I don't see much nature."

I said, "I get it. I suggest you watch Dewitt Jones's TEDx talk 'Celebrate What's Right with the World!' and subscribe to his free daily images. It's a way to get out in nature without getting up from your chair."

Dewitt shares a wonderful story at the end of his presentation. He's on a professional shoot and it's "one of those days" where everything's going wrong. The light is off and none of the images are popping. On top of the day's frustrations is the fact that a little boy has attached himself to Dewitt, pestering him with questions. Every time Dewitt sets up for a shot, the little boy steps in front of his tripod and snaps the same picture with his little pink plastic camera.

Dewitt is getting a bit annoyed. Then, the little boy, Adam, looks up at Dewitt and asks, "Do you have a camera?"

Well, as Dewitt says, he's *festooned* with expensive camera equipment of every kind. He answers impatiently, "Yes."

Adam pauses and then says, "Yeah, but does yours have juice in it?"

Busted. No, as Dewitt says, he didn't have juice in his camera. The little boy did. At that moment, Dewitt was looking at the world with exasperated eyes. The little boy was looking at the world with awe-inspired eyes.

There Is No Present Like the Time

"What a wonderful life I've had. I only wish I'd realized it sooner."
—Colette

If you want to be happier, follow Adam's example and look at the world with juice in your eyes.

Many of us live under constant time pressure. Our days are ruled by the clock. We get up at a certain time. Go to work at a certain time. Have meals and appointments at a certain time. We often run late, which causes us to fall behind, and this causes us to feel behind. And when we feel behind, it can feel like we're failing.

Do you feel the "hurrier you go, the behinder you get"? As you've probably discovered, it's hard to be happy when you're hurried. Fortunately, there is a way to counteract this hurry sickness that has such a devastating effect on our quality of life.

There is no present like the time—and no time like the present—to get out of your head and "calm to your senses." You can do it with this simple "I See Now" exercise.

1. **Look around and let your eyes settle on one specific thing.** Make it for your eyes only. Really look at the chair you're sitting on. Feel the fabric, bounce on the cushion, examine the construction. Think of all the hours you've sat there, all the experiences you've had there. What you didn't notice seconds before can become a source of intrigue.
2. **Gaze at something else in your vicinity and examine it closely.** Is there a computer or phone nearby? Chances are you turn it on and use it without even thinking about what a miracle it is to tap on a piece of plastic and instantly transmit a message to someone thousands of miles away. Really study this inanimate object. Think about the ideas you've created, the laughs you've shared, the connections you've experienced. It's impossible to take this device for granted if you really see it for the miracle it is.

3. **Move your eyes to someone in the area.** Instead of looking at this person and seeing only the "story" you know about him or her based on your history ("She doesn't listen to me." "He forgot to get gas in the car again." "Why did she get that promotion and I didn't?"), look at that person with fresh eyes. Imagine you're meeting him or her for the first time. Does it help you see them with more empathetic eyes?

The Power of the "I See Now" Exercise to Change Your Mood

"God can really show off when she wants to."

— ANNE LAMOTT

There are many benefits to this "I See Now" exercise. Not only does it help us unplug from our digital devices so we can be present instead of perpetually preoccupied, it can lift our spirits when we're feeling down.

I met a friend for a long overdue lunch at a restaurant nestled at the foot of a magnificent mountain range. Over our meal, she told me how sad she was about still being single in her forties. "I always thought I'd meet the right guy someday, marry, and have a family. Looks like that's not going to happen and there's nothing I can do about it."

I didn't want to trivialize her problem, however I knew she had good things going on in her life that she was overlooking. I also thought her expression and body posture were contributing to her depression. Her face was slack and she was slumped in her chair, eyes cast downward. I said, "Look up. Don't say anything. Just gaze around and take it all in."

She sat back in her chair and slowly swept the landscape with her eyes. After a moment, she looked at me questioningly. I said, "Tell me what you saw."

"Well, the mountains."

I interrupted, "Tell me in detail what you just saw."

"Well, banana trees, mango trees, avocado, and green pineapple fields extending up into the hills . . ." and she continued to recount what she'd just seen.

I asked, "How do you feel now?"

She thought about it for a moment and then smiled, "Better."

Exactly. You've heard the expression, "Things are looking up?" That's not just an expression, it's a prescription. You can lift your spirits by lifting your eyes. You can elevate your mood by elevating your gaze. Simply said, it's hard to feel down when you're looking up. Try it right where you are, right now. Lift your head. Lift your eyes. Look around and really see things as if for the first or last time. How do you feel? Hopefully, better.

And if you feel a need for green but can't find any, visit Discover TheForest.org. I first heard about this on an Ad Council "Get Out in Your Naturehood" radio campaign. It's very cool. Put your zip code in the website's search engine and up will come nature outings within a five- to fifty-mile radius. It even has an "Every Kid in a Park" feature and a geo-triggered app called "Agents of Discovery," which gamifies your outdoor adventures. Great for family outings.

A woman emailed, "I'm housebound. Getting out in nature is not an option. Suggestions?"

I responded, "Ask someone to bring you some flowers. It doesn't even have to be a bouquet. A single flower can be more beautiful than a bunch. Put that flower by your bed so it's the first thing you see in the morning and the last thing you see at night."

And if you don't have the budget for, or access to, flowers, upload a screen-saver program that shows nature's wonders so every time you look at your computer screen, you're taking a trip around the world and experiencing her beauties. And be sure to subscribe to Dewitt's daily images so you can steep yourself in Mother Nature's abundance without leaving home.

The point of this chapter? Part of turning a *Someday into a Today* is to notice what's right, right here, right now. The happiness we seek is available anytime we want . . . for a moment's *notice*.

15

Get a Move On

"To me, life boils down to one thing, it's movement."

—JERRY SEINFELD

I wrapped up a presentation in Portland, Oregon, and was on my way to dinner with my host. We needed to navigate some dark steps down to the hotel parking lot. I peered into the abyss and reached for a handrail, but there wasn't one. I took what I thought was the last step, fell, and crashed ribs-first into a parked car.

I sat there, stunned, in a state of shock. One minute I was fine, the next minute I wasn't. My friend asked anxiously, "Are you okay?"

"I think so. I just need to walk it off." That had always been my strategy. When I played league tennis, if I twisted my ankle, I knew to stay on my feet and keep walking. If I sat down, the injury set in. As long as I kept moving, my body would somehow, miraculously, heal itself.

So, I walked around until I felt "myself" again. At dinner, my ribs were sore, but I didn't think much of it until the next morning when I woke up and couldn't get out of bed. My whole side was on fire. Any sudden movement brought a gasp of pain. I gingerly levered myself out of bed, crawled to my laptop, googled my symptoms, and determined I had bruised or cracked ribs. (Side note: Yes, I know doctors really don't like it when we use Dr. Google to self-diagnose.)

WebMD said that if I went to the ER, they'd take X-rays to see if I was in danger of puncturing a lung, but otherwise wouldn't even "tape me up," as physicians now feel that outdated practice hurts more than it helps. They would, perhaps, give me pain meds and advise me to "take it easy." As long as I didn't aggravate the injury, the ribs would eventually knit back together.

Hmm. I was flying to Hawaii later that day. Perhaps this was naïve, but I decided I might as well take it easy in the islands. I gingerly headed to the airport and discovered that as long as I walked slowly without swinging my arms, it didn't hurt too much. It was only when I needed to lift anything, such as my carry-on suitcase, that my body quickly reminded me, "*Don't* do that!"

I arrived safe (but not so sound) and checked into a lovely hotel in Wailea. The only drawback? It was modern which meant everything was low. Low couches. Low chairs. Low beds. I looked at the bed and wondered how I was ever going to get in it, much less out of it.

I thought, "I know. I'll go for a walk on the beach path." I had spent hundreds of happy hours traversing that path when we lived in that area, and as mentioned, walking was my cure-all.

Good idea in theory, not so much in practice. Five minutes into my walk, I knew it was a mistake. The narrow, winding path was crowded with runners, speed walkers, and baby strollers, which meant I was dodging someone or something every other minute. Not an option. I headed back to the hotel, feeling like a wimp.

Are You a Participant or a Spectator?

"Do something today your future self will thank you for."
— SIGN IN A GYM

So, what happened? I became a spectator. I sat and looked at the ocean and didn't even dip my toes in. I watched people swim, snorkel, and sail and didn't get up from my chair. I watched people being active, yet I felt distant from them. It was like I had retreated from life.

And you know what I learned? There is a slippery slope between being a participant *in* life and being a spectator *of* life. I'm normally an active person, but here I was sitting on the sidelines. And the longer I sat, the less I felt like doing anything.

Remember the Law of Inertia? A stationary body tends to stay stationary? A body in motion tends to stay in motion? I discovered, and not in a good way, the stultifying effects of being sedentary. The word "stultifying" means "cause to lose enthusiasm and initiative." That's what happened to me. I watched people going about their lives but felt removed from them and unmoved by them. It made me feel apart from life instead of feeling a part of life.

It was perfectly sunny outside, but I was gloomy inside. One morning I got fed up with the doldrums and thought, "I've got to *do* something about this," so I got up, got outside, got moving. Things instantly got better. I realized, "Movement = mood. The more sedentary I am, the more depressed I am. The more active I am, the more energized I am."

I lucked out because the hotel had a walk-in pool with a gentle entry slope so I didn't have to climb up and down a ladder to get in and out. Immersing myself in that water was like coming home. It felt so good to be back in my element. I gently treaded water and moved my arms in circular infinity loops. I could almost feel my ribs healing. What bliss to be back in motion.

Are You Grateful for Your Health or Taking It for Granted?

> "If I knew I was going to live this long,
> I would have taken better care of myself."
>
> — MICKEY MANTLE

How about you? Are you in good health? Free from aches, pains, illness? Are you grateful for it or taking it for granted?

Think back to the Happiness Interview where you listed your top five priorities. Was health in your top five? The question is, was it also in the top five things you spend the most time on?

For many of us, it's not. Our health is an afterthought. We *know* we should get up off the couch or out from behind that desk and get a move on—but it keeps getting squeezed out of our busy life. We take our health for granted—until something goes wrong.

The purpose of this chapter is to remind us that if we want to live a long time, *now* is the time to take better care of ourselves. Happiness and health go hand in hand. How will you use your freedom of movement *before* you lose it? How will you be a participant, not a spectator?

After two weeks of healing in Hawaii, I returned to my Year by the Water travels on the Mainland. I was driving through the Great Smoky Mountains listening to Garrison Keillor's final show of *A Prairie Home Companion*, broadcast live from the Hollywood Bowl. President Obama called in to give Keillor a well-deserved shout-out for his forty-two years (!) of story-telling that, as Obama put it, "made us all a little more humane."

Obama kept trying to focus the conversation on Keillor. Keillor kept turning it back to Obama. Keillor asked, "What are you looking forward to when you're out of office?"

Obama didn't even have to think about it. He laughed. "Getting in a car without the Secret Service and going for a drive."

Exactly. Getting in a car and going where we want, when we want, is the epitome of freedom. Yet many of us don't even think about it, much less value it.

As Abraham Maslow pointed out in his Hierarchy of Needs, "Satisfied needs are no longer motivators." In other words, once we have food, safety, shelter, and our freedoms, we tend to overlook them. We don't miss them until we lose them.

Are You Taking Your Freedoms for Granted?

"Do any human beings ever realize life while they live it?"
—THORNTON WILDER, *OUR TOWN*

Freedom, in all its forms, is far too precious to take for granted. This was brought home by an incident that happened during a holiday vacation in California's Yosemite Valley.

We were staying at a family lodge that featured snowshoeing and sledding. We lived in Hawaii at the time, so playing in the snow was a big draw for Tom and Andrew. What we hadn't counted on was the blizzard that kept us inside. No worries, there was ping-pong and board games so we were happy campers.

One night, the manager confided he was concerned about a couple who had not checked in. He didn't know if they'd gotten lost in the blizzard, gone off the road into a snow bank, or what.

Suddenly, the door blew open and the couple staggered in. We gathered round to find out what had happened. Yes, they'd gotten lost, but here's the part that made a lasting impression on me: they hadn't panicked because *they were in the United States.*

They had grown up in Russia. If they wanted to travel internally, they had to give authorities their itinerary. If they didn't arrive at each checkpoint by a certain time, they came under suspicion and could be interrogated, even arrested. The couple told us they hadn't worried because they had food, water, blankets, and trusted that they'd be safe until someone rescued them. At least they didn't have to worry about being tossed in jail and losing their freedom.

Their story had an enduring impact on me. I promised to realize what it meant to have freedom of movement instead of being nonchalant about what a blessing it is.

Are You Making the Most of Your Freedom of Movement?

"After one has been in prison, it is the small things one appreciates:
being able to take a walk whenever one wants, going into a shop and
buying a newspaper, speaking or choosing to remain silent.
The simple act of being able to control one's person."
— NELSON MANDELA

When I remember what it was like not being able to walk without
pain, when I reflect on what it was like traversing the country with
complete freedom and without fear, I am reminded all over again that
mobility is too special to take casually.

Think about it. Many of us never give a *moment's notice* to what it
means to be able to get in a car and go where we want, when we want.
We fall into mind-numbing routines, commute to work the same way
every day and run errands, many times on congested roads and in
bumper-to-bumper traffic. We see transportation as a source of frustration, not as a source of freedom.

How about changing that this weekend? Cars, bikes, feet, trains,
subways, planes aren't just a tool for transportation; they can be a tool
for transformation. Stop taking the freedom of movement they grant
us for granted. Start seeing them as a happiness facilitator.

Is there a place in your area that you've always wanted to explore,
but for whatever reason, haven't? It could be a historical landmark, a different section of town, a scenic spot. Put a date on the calendar for
getting yourself there. If you don't have a car and it's too far to walk,
rent a ZipCar, take a train or subway, hop on the bus, jump on your bike.

But this time, instead of trying to get from Point A to Point B as
fast as you can, appreciate the fact that you're free to travel where you
want without having to get permission, without having to report your
destination to the authorities, and without having to arrive by a certain
time or you could land in jail. Revel in the autonomy you have to "make
it up as you go."

I'm not the only one who feels mobility is the quintessence of autonomy. This was brought home while I was in Austin, Texas, speaking at SXSW. The keynoter that morning was Logan Green, founder of LYFT. He updated us on trends in the industry and said rather matter-of-factly, "Self-driving cars will become the norm in our lifetime."

His interviewer was incredulous. He said, "I was born and raised in Texas. From the time I was fourteen, all my friends and I did was think about cars, talk about cars, and save money to buy our first car. The day we turned sixteen, we were first in line at the Department of Motor Vehicles applying for a driver's license." He stopped and then said, as if he still couldn't quite believe it, "My son, who is eighteen, doesn't even want a car. He's not even planning on getting his driver's license. What a change in a single generation."

As he talked, I noticed the woman next to me had tears in her eyes. I asked, "Are you okay?"

"All I can think about is my dad. We had to take his keys away from him last month. It was heartbreaking, the hardest thing I've ever had to do. He's eighty years old. His vision is going and he's on medication, but he fought us every step of the way. He sees this as losing his independence and is afraid it's going to be all downhill from here."

Why am I sharing this? Because we don't want to wait until we lose our "license to drive" to value our mobility, independence, and freedom of movement. If you've ever thought about taking a road trip, now might be the time. And it doesn't have to be cross-country or cross state, it can be across the county line. The goal is to revel in your autonomy and appreciate what a privilege it is to get in a car and go wherever you want to go.

Walking Is a Moving Form of Mindfulness

"Walk as if you are kissing the earth with your feet."
—THICH NHAT HANH

There is another way to value our freedom of movement. And it's not power walking.

Please understand, I believe in power walks. For the first few decades of my life, I was a runner, competitive swimmer, and tennis player. The goal of exercise was to push myself, get my heart rate up, and, no matter what, *not stop*. As the gym-rat saying goes, "Sweat is fat crying."

Stopping was for wimps, wusses. But while recovering from my hurt ribs, I got into strolling and stopping. I have longtime friend Judy Gray to thank for giving me clarity about that. Judy was CEO of the Florida Society for Association Executives. It was time to explore Florida on my Year by the Water so we agreed to meet at the historic Vinoy Park Hotel in St. Petersburg.

Judy knew about my ribs so we took . . . our . . . time. We wandered, meandered, and literally stopped to smell the roses. Judy laughed. "This is like going for a walk with my dogs. They turn every walk into an exploration. Tails up. Eyes bright. Sniff. Sniff. It doesn't matter if they've seen our street a thousand times before, it's still intriguing to them." She added, "You know, we don't really experience a place until we walk it."

Judy's right. At that point, I had crisscrossed the country from Marina Del Rey to Chesapeake Bay . . . twice. I'd had the pleasure of staying at waterfront towns from Pensacola to Portland, the Hawaiian Islands to Hilton Head Island. What she said was true. I could *see* a town by driving through. But I didn't really connect with it unless I explored it on my own two feet. It's the difference between being an observer and a doer.

So, I will continue to power walk to get my heart pumping, my blood flowing, and my body moving. But I will also kiss the earth with my feet, and be mindful of my surroundings with a dog's always-alert eyes and appreciative heart. I will walk and roll *and* stop and stroll.

Meditate on the Move

"If in doubt, walk until your day becomes interesting."

—ROLF POTTS

How about you? What does walking mean *to* you and do *for* you? Does it help you appreciate your autonomy? Counteract being a couch or desk potato?

I agree with travel blogger Rolf Potts about the power of using walking as a creative act. I have *never* gone for a walk without seeing something interesting, which causes me to think something interesting, which causes my life to be more interesting. And an interesting life is a happy life.

When will you get outside, revel in your freedom of movement and "kiss the earth" with your feet? When will you go for a walk to create a more interesting life?

In the next chapter, you'll discover why even if you're busy, especially if you're busy, it's not frivolous to have fun; it's a prescription for a more fulfilling life.

16

Free Up Time for Fun

"Everything works better if you unplug it for a few minutes. Including you."

—ANNE LAMOTT

While in Costa Rica at a conference for transformational leaders, I had breakfast with Dr. Ivan Misner and his wife Beth. Ivan founded BNI, one of the world's largest networking organizations.

While getting caught up, I told them about all the different business activities I had going on. Ivan said, "Sam, sounds like a full calendar. What do you do for fun?"

I told him, "I agree with Stephen King who said, 'I have the world's best job. I get paid to hang out in my imagination all day. That's what I get to do and it's fun for me.'"

He paused, then said, "Sam, I think you're dodging the question. What do you do *just for fun?*"

Long pause. I finally came up with, "Hmmm, well, I walk my dog around the lake."

He just looked at me. He didn't even have to say anything. Even I knew that was a pathetic answer.

I'm not alone in being too busy to have fun. In her excellent book *Overwhelmed*, Brigid Schulte cites a variety of studies in which people report they're "too busy to vote, make friends outside the office, sleep, have lunch, even too busy to have sex."

Why are we doing this to ourselves? Why, when someone asks, "How are you doing?" is the first word out of our mouth often . . . "*Busy.*"

Is it a high? It is because we need to feel productive, important, useful? Is it because we feel a responsibility to our employer, employees, and customers?

Probably all of that. But there's something else going on. Some of us are afraid to have fun. It seems frivolous. Indulgent. Like we don't have anything "better" to do with our time.

Is Work Running Your Life?

"Of all the things that really and truly matter,
getting more done is not one of them."

— MIKE DOOLEY

Somewhere along the line we got the message that fun is something we do only when our work is done. Since, for many of us, our work is never done, that leaves no time for fun.

Some people call this the Puritan or Protestant Work Ethic which is loosely defined as the belief that our worth as a human being is proportionate to how hard we work. As Dan Pollota pointed out in a *Harvard Business Review* article entitled "Worry Isn't Work," "We . . . correlate our sense of responsibility . . . with how hard we are being on ourselves." That may sound innocent, but it is ultimately toxic because it means our work ethic determines whether we feel we've *earned* the right to have fun and be happy.

Sound like anyone you know?

All I know is that the conscious or subconscious belief that "Work is the holy grail and the secret sauce to success" is having a deterimental effect on our health, relationships, and quality of life.

That is not just my opinion. Study after study shows the devastating impact of working long hours, taking work home with us, of being so consumed with our job that "52 percent of us don't take our full paid vacation." I'm not making that up. That's a confirmed statistic reported by CNBC.

A Time.com article by *Barking Up the Wrong Tree* blogger, Eric Barker, featured many psychologists who reported their burned-out clients can't shake the notion that the "busier they are, the more they're thought of as competent, smart, successful, admired, even envied."

The toll of that kind of thinking? Dr. Ed Hallowell, author of *Driven to Distraction*, says he's witnessed an upsurge of the number of people who complain of being chronically inattentive, disorganized, and overbooked. Many come to him wondering if they have ADHD. He says, "While some do, most do not. Instead, they have what I call a severe case of modern life."

What I know now is that—before I launched my Year by the Water—I must have had a case of "modern life," because it seemed I never had any leftover "bandwidth" for fun.

Is Fun Something You Do When All Your Work Is Done?

*"Never underestimate the importance of having fun. I am going
to have fun every day I have left. You have to decide
whether you're a Tigger or an Eeyore."*

— RANDY PAUSCH

The answer to this? Free up time for fun. Play dates aren't just for kids. Get crystal clear about what makes you laugh and enjoy your life, and schedule it on your calendar.

To help you do that—because it may mean overcoming years of

habitual workaholism—I've curated a few favorite quotes about the importance of enjoying life.

Pick one of these (or a favorite from previous pages) and post it where you'll see it every day. The next time you're about to postpone that date night, family vacation, or call to your folks because you're overloaded with work, ask yourself, "What will matter in the long run?"

The next time you're about to back out of a walk in a park or a concert with friends because you're "too busy," look at your quote and honor that play date. Remember the saying from years ago, "No one on his deathbed ever said, 'I wish I'd spent more time at work'?" Keep that in mind the next time you're about to postpone something enjoyable you'll regret not doing.

> "Life is too short to live the same day twice."
>
> —JENNIFER LOPEZ

> "If you can laugh at it, you can live with it."
>
> —ERMA BOMBECK

> "It is a happy talent to know how to play."
>
> —RALPH WALDO EMERSON

> "If at the end of the day I can say I've had fun, it was a good day."
>
> —SIMONE BILES

> "If you are losing your leisure, look out, you may be losing your soul."
>
> —LOGAN P. SMITH

> "Laughter is the shortest distance between two people."
>
> —VICTOR BORGE

> "For fast-acting relief, try slowing down."
>
> —LILY TOMLIN

"A woman can best refind herself by losing herself in some kind of
creative activity of her own."
— ANNE MORROW LINDBERGH

"I told the doctor I couldn't relax. He said, 'Force yourself.'"
— LEN DETTINGER

What are You Going to Say YES To?

"The big question is whether you are going to be
able say a hearty YES to your adventure."
—JOSEPH CAMPBELL

While speaking to a group of contractors in Hawaii, a woman stood up in our conference session and said, "We don't do *vacations*, we do *conventions*."

The rest of the audience laughed in recognition of that truth and then chimed in with their own stories. Many were in their fifties and sixties. They had thriving businesses, but no succession plan and felt they couldn't retire because they had so many people counting on them.

We brainstormed ways to work smarter, not harder, so it's not all work and no play. I recommended several resources that show how to triage your time and talent so you're not doing it all yourself, including Michael Gerber's classic *The E-Myth* series, which asks the compelling question, "Are you working *on* your business or *in* your business?"

A contractor stood up and said, "I am definitely working *in* my business, not *on* it. I always thought my two sons would take over my company when I was ready to call it quits, but they're not interested, and, frankly, I wouldn't want to burden them with the stress."

I told him, "I met Mike Michalowicz at SXSW. He travels around the world sharing his 'Toilet Paper Entrepreneur' strategies for how to build a life, not just a business. He told me, 'Many people want to be an entrepreneur so they can be their own boss. But they don't end up being their own boss. Their business ends up being the boss.'"

I told the group, "Work isn't supposed to be a nonstop grindstone. If we don't have time to say yes to adventures that energize us and keep us healthy, we're doing it wrong. It's worth checking out Mike's books so you're no longer a slave to what he calls the 'Sell It, Do It' cycle."

How about you? Is your career running you or are you running your career? There's a short answer to that. If you don't have time for fun, if you frequently cancel commitments with friends, family, or hobbies because you've "got work to do," then your career is running you.

When Was the Last Time You Had Fun?

"The standard of success in life isn't the things . . .
the money or the stuff. It is absolutely the amount of joy that you feel."
— ESTHER HICKS

A thirty-something techie named Ben told me. "I work in Silicon Valley. It's almost a badge of honor to talk about how long it's been since you've had a day off. If you walk into offices around here, you'll see walls covered with posters that say, 'Rise and grind,' 'Good things may come to those who wait, but only the things left by those who hustle,' 'Nothing worth having comes easy,' 'While you're off relaxing, the guy working weekends will beat your ass and win.'

"I bought into the grind mentality until my girlfriend broke up with me. I had cancelled out on her so many times she got fed up and left. It's too late to get her back, but it forced me to rethink what I was doing. My plan was to work hard until I made my 'number,' then kick back and reap the rewards. I realized I was throwing everyone under the bus while I did that and it wasn't worth it.

"A friend told me about Zogsports. Their motto is 'Play like you did when you were a kid.' I played Little League growing up and was on my high-school baseball team. It's been years since I've played competitively, and most of my skills are long gone, but I can still play softball. It gets me out of the office at a decent hour a couple times a week and it's fun. I play on a co-ed team so I'm actually meeting people outside work. Who knows? Maybe even a new girlfriend. I wish I had done this a long time ago."

How about you? Do you swap jokes about "hump day," "Thank God it's Friday" and "It's been a long, hard week and it's only Monday," but keep doing it instead of doing something about it?

If so, perhaps it's time to update the phrase "take time *off* work."

Stop Thinking of Fun as Taking Time *Off*

"If you want things to be different, perhaps the answer is to be different yourself."

—Norman Vincent Peale

Larry, a contractor at that conference in Maui, asked, "So, what was un-expected about your Year by the Water?"

I told him, "How many people are working themselves to death. That's not just an observation. A 2015 *Atlantic* article by Gillian B. White reported that work-related stress is now the number five killer in the United States, and that 'health problems associated with job-related anxiety account for more deaths each year than Alzheimer's or diabetes.'"

Larry said, "I thought it was just our industry. I had no idea it was that bad."

"I saw firsthand that many people are leading a life that will lead to regrets. It shouldn't be work hard until we're sixty-five, retire, and *then* be happy. I think that model is broken."

"What do you mean?"

"I used to speak on cruise ships. It was sad to see the disproportion-ate number of female widows on the ship. Many had similar stories. They and their husbands had worked hard and saved their money for retirement with the hopes of enjoying their golden years together. But that's not what happened. The male spouse died shortly after retiring. The widow was left with time, money, but not the person she wanted to cruise with. Their regrets and wished-for 'do-overs' clarified for me that life isn't supposed to be work now, play later. It's supposed to be a blend of both now."

Larry said, "Easier said than done, Sam. Most of us in this industry have a payroll to meet. We have employees depending on us, clients relying on us. We can't tell them, 'I'm out of here and go gallivanting across the country.' That would be irresponsible."

"I understand. I'm not suggesting you *abandon* your obligations; I'm suggesting you *balance* them. Yes, you have a responsibility to your employees and clients, and you also have a responsibility to yourself. Scheduling time every week to do something that makes you happier and healthier sets a positive precedent for all involved. You're showing by example that *you matter*, and that means not working yourself to death.

"You don't have to take my word for this. A *Fast Company* article entitled "Why Happy Employees Are 12% More Productive" cites studies that show that 'we work more effectively, creatively and collaboratively when we're happy at work.' These studies show it pays to play, that people who enjoy their work are more loyal and take fewer sick days. Fun isn't a nicety; it's a necessity. It's a bottom-line win for all involved to build play into your personal and professional life."

Larry pushed back, "I agree with that in theory; it's hard to do in practice."

"That's why it's so important to change how we talk about this. Albert Einstein said we can't solve a problem with the same thinking that caused it. Well, we can't solve this problem with the same *language* that caused it. As long as we think of having fun and taking vacations as taking time *off* work, we see them as an *exception* to to the rule. Let's frame fun and vacations around what we *are* doing instead of what we're *not*. Instead of seeing them as taking time off work, see them as taking time on life. You're not taking time *away* from your job, you're investing time *in* your well-being."

Get out your calendar right now. Schedule two "play times" this month so they don't get squeezed out of your life. Start imagining your

W's—*Where* you'll go, *Who* you'll be with, and *What* fun you'll have—to ramp up your anticipation and enthusiasm.

And when the time comes and your "to-do's" tempt you to back out, remind yourself you'll never get it all done, you'll never be all caught up. Honor the play date. Your well-being will thank you for it.

And if you think you can't afford to do the things that make you happy, please rethink that. As you'll discover next, *meaning* makes us happy, not *money*. And everyone can afford that.

17

Be Wealthy in What Matters

"I wish everyone could get rich and famous . . .
so they will know it's not the answer."

—Jim Carrey

was in Boulder to help Tom's wife, Patty, with the kids while he went to *Mars*. Well, MDRS (Mars Desert Research Station in Utah) . . . as close as you can get to Mars while on Earth.

Here's the backstory.

The Mars Society had called to ask Tom if he'd like to head up an international team for a two-week mission at the Mars biosphere in the Utah desert. Would he?! Tom grew up reading sci-fi, space exploration thrillers by Isaac Asimov, Ray Bradbury, and Ben Bova. This was his dream.

After months of planning calls and online coordination, the big day finally came for Tom to drive to Utah. And everything that could go wrong did. A crucial task was still incomplete. A team member's flight was delayed. Another team member had forgotten an important item and Tom was frantically trying to track it down.

It took several hours to solve the last-minute crises, which made

Tom late. He grabbed his bags, gave Patty a quick peck on the cheek, hugged the kids, and started racing out the door.

I called after him, "Tom, stop."

He turned and looked at me, impatient to get going, "What?"

"This moment is too important to miss. Think back. You're the eight-year-old boy who, when I asked, 'What do you want to be when you grow up?' pointed to the sky and said, 'Something to do with up there.'

"You're the teenager who was thrilled to get into Virginia Tech so you could study aerospace engineering, astronomy, math, and physics and whose college team won the International Competition to put a Manned Mission on Mars.

"You're the twenty-something who was hired by NASA to work in Mission Control at Johnson Space Center with the International Space Station.

"Take a moment to look around and imprint this. You're married to your soul mate. You're blessed with two happy, healthy children. *Your dreams have come true.*"

Tom did look around. He did imprint. In fact, do you remember the famous *Life* magazine photo of the sailor kissing a nurse on the streets of Manhattan to celebrate the end of World War II? Tom did his own version of that and swept Patty up in a wildly romantic kiss to celebrate the occasion. *That's* being wealthy in what matters.

Has Your Dream Come True and You're Not Even Noticing It?

"Not everything that can be counted counts,
and not everything that counts can be counted."

— ALBERT EINSTEIN

Why did I share Tom's story? Because Einstein was right. What counts can't be counted. But it can be noticed, appreciated, and imprinted.

Many people have told me they're not happy because they have money problems. They tell me they'll be happy when they get a raise, have more savings in the bank, or pay off their debt. They think they'll be happy when they can buy a bigger house, fancier car, better clothes, or nicer toys.

And certainly, money matters. Just ask a friend who has a Go-FundMe campaign to help pay for medical costs and an expensive surgery for a brain tumor that is jeopardizing her life.

Just ask out-of-work individuals who have mounting bills and who haven't been able to find a job no matter how many résumés they send out. Just ask young people who can't attend college because they don't qualify for a scholarship or a loan and can't afford tuition.

So, money matters. But it is not the key to happiness. That's not just my opinion. Studies have shown there's a certain "number" people need to be happy. And the number is $75,000.

I'm not making that up. A survey by the Gallup World Poll of more than 1.7 million people from 164 countries found that "people are happiest when they make between $60,000 and $75,000 a year." *What is surprising is that earning more than this "threshold amount" can actually result in lower overall life satisfaction.* I'll say that again because it flies in the face of what many people think. *More money does not equal more happiness.*

What Does Money Mean to You?

"Money can't buy me love."

— PAUL MCCARTNEY

There are many theories about why "money can't buy happiness." The Hedonic Treadmill is a psychological phenomenon that states we pursue pleasurable things—wealth, status, fame, stuff—in the mistaken belief they'll make us happy. When we finally achieve or acquire them, they're nice for a while, but then "the thrill is gone" and we're on to the "next new thing" in a never-ceasing search for contentment. That perpetual cycle results in a "never *have* enough, never *feel* we're enough" emptiness.

You may have heard of the curse of lottery winners. "About

70 percent of people who suddenly receive a windfall of cash will lose it within a few years," according to the National Endowment for Financial Education.

A surprising amount of winners say *they wish it had never happened.* Jack Whittaker, who won $315 million in a West Virginia Lottery, said, "I wish we had torn the ticket up." Abraham Shakespeare, who won a $30 million lotto, said, "I would have been better off broke."

Donna Mikkin, who won $34.5 million in the 2007 New York State Lottery, said her financial windfall ruined her life and led to emotional bankruptcy. "Most of us think that winning the lottery is the ultimate fulfillment. We see it as some magic pot of gold waiting for us at the end of the rainbow. If you ask me, my life was hijacked by the lottery."

Those laments from lottery winners riled up a salon attendee, Will, who said, "Give me a winning ticket to a lottery. I'll be the exception to this rule and prove we *can* be rich and happy. The only people who think money doesn't matter are the ones who have it."

I told him, "Point taken. You're right, money can contribute to our quality of life, and there are people who are rich and happy. It's also important to understand that while money can buy *the* good life, it can't buy *a* good life."

"What do you mean by that?"

"Years ago, I had an opportunity to speak at an international gathering of the Young Presidents' Organization. The opening keynote speaker was Notre Dame professor Tom Morris. Tom skipped perfunctory remarks and jumped right in with a question: 'What does it mean to live *the* good life? Shout out your answers.' Members of the audience called out, 'Money. Fame. Success. Travel. Good food.' Someone called out, 'Bali' and everyone laughed."

He continued, "Okay, what's it mean to live *a* good life?" The answers instantly changed. "Integrity. Wisdom. Legacy. Health. Values, Family."

In sixty seconds, Tom had introduced a provocative and profound concept. The all-important difference between living *the* good life or *a* good life. Or, what the Greeks call "eudaimonia," which means "human flourishing, prosperity, virtuous excellence."

Are You Leading A Good Life or *The* Good Life?

"Money doesn't guarantee happiness; it guarantees options."
— CHRIS ROCK

How about you? How would *you* answer those questions? How would you differentiate between *the* good life and *a* good life?

What role does money play in your life satisfaction? Are you happy or unhappy with the amount of money you have, make, save, invest, give? If so, how so? If not, why not? What's your "number"? How much more do you need to have the quality of life you want?

While writing this chapter, I watched a sobering E:60 documentary on ESPN about former NFL quarterback Ryan Leaf. You may remember Ryan as an exciting college player who competed with Peyton Manning to be the #1 pick in the 1998 National Football League draft. Ryan was picked second by the San Diego Chargers and signed to a four-year, $31 million-dollar contract, with a guaranteed signing bonus of $11 million, the largest ever paid to a rookie at the time.

Unfortunately, fame and fortune did not lead to happiness. His substance abuse and addiction to painkillers led to a felony burglary that landed him in prison. His cellmate encouraged him to get clean and share his story with others. He now travels the country speaking to schools and organizations about his lessons learned. He ended this eye-opening interview by saying, "I was making $5 million a year in the NFL and was miserable. When I started working for Transcend Recovery Community, I was making $15 an hour and *I'd never been happier in my life.*"

The day after watching that documentary was Easter Sunday, and I explored the waterfront here in Morro Bay. Three of the more famous restaurants were packed with lines out the door. People were standing around waiting, not too patiently. I couldn't help but overhear conversations as I walked by, "What's taking so long?! Our reservation was for half an hour ago!" "Bethany, stop whining. You're driving me nuts." None of these people looked happy. They looked annoyed, angry, disconnected. No one seemed to be having a good time.

A few hundred yards away was a lovely waterside park with a whale-tail slide in a playground. Several families had spread out blankets and set up a circle of camp chairs. They were chowing down on tri-tip, throwing balls for dogs, strumming guitars, playing catch, and talking story. They looked relaxed, connected with one another, and like they were genuinely enjoying themselves.

I thought, "Hmmm, those people back at the famous restaurants will probably drop $200 to $300 for a fancy meal and they're miserable. People here probably paid $20 to $30 to bring something to the potluck and they're having a wonderful time. *The* good life. *A* good life. Choose."

As my friend Dianne the psychologist says, "Do you know how children spell love? T-I-M-E." This weekend, spend *time* with people you care about. You don't have to spend money to have a good time, to have a good life. Happiness doesn't have to cost a thing. Give your loved ones your attention—your ears and your eyes. That will be enough.

Is It Time to Switch Your Story About Money?

> "My favorite things in life don't cost any money. It's really clear that the most precious resource we all have is time."
>
> —STEVE JOBS

The Washington Post used to feature a column called *Life Is Short* in which readers summed up their life story in under one hundred words. My all-time favorite, James Boeringer (who looked to be about eighty years old in his photo), said, "I'm getting on, but I still find ways to be useful.

"For example, this morning I noticed our salt was in the shaker with the little holes and the pepper was in the shaker with the big holes. I got two pieces of clean paper and emptied the salt onto one and the pepper onto the other. Then I funneled the condiments into the appropriate containers without spilling any. My wife was watching. When I finished, she asked, *'Why didn't you just switch the caps?'*"

Arggh. Is it time to switch a story you have about money?

If you perceive you don't have enough to be happy, could you rethink that? Could you realize the happiness you seek doesn't have to cost a thing; it's available right here, right now—for free and for a moment's notice?

Have some of your dreams come true and you're not even noticing them?

Are you already wealthy in what matters, rich in what counts?

Are you already leading *a* good life?

In the next chapter, you'll discover another way to be wealthy in what matters by creating a "rising tide raising all involved" community and by AFFILATING with people who want the best for you and who bring out the best in you.

LIFE HACK 6

AFFILIATE with People Who Have Your Back and Front

"Anything is possible if you have the right people supporting you."

— MISTY COPELAND

EVALUATE

RELOCATE   GENERATE

INNOVATE   ABDICATE

NEGOTIATE   INITIATE

INTEGRATE   CELEBRATE

AFFILIATE

Life Hack 6 shows how to AFFILIATE with people who support your Top Priorities, expedite their success, and make them even more rewarding. You'll also discover why "only" doesn't have to be "lonely" and how to create meaningful connections wherever you go so you can create a community of one or one hundred.

18

Launch Your Ship in Public

"When you're surrounded by people who share a
passionate commitment around a common purpose,
anything is possible."

—HOWARD SCHULTZ

The Central Coast Writers Conference invited me to deliver their
opening keynote and hosted me at a shorefront hotel. The morning before my keynote, I went for a walk-talk to Morro Rock (a
581-foot volcanic plug landmark that can be seen from miles away) to
mentally rehearse my presentation. As I walked along the bay, I noticed
some people pointing toward the mouth of the harbor. Curious, I walked
over and asked, "What's going on?"

A man turned and said, "Oh, the *San Salvador* is arriving this morning. It's a replica ship on its maiden voyage up the coast. It's supposed
to be arriving any minute."

Talk about dots connecting. Part of my morning ritual is to listen
to Colin Hay, in particular his song "Waiting for My Real Life to Begin" with its cautionary lyrics about the perils of waiting for our ship
to come in. I jogged to the point, peering through what the locals call a

"marine layer" for a glimpse of the ship. There it was, emerging from the fog. I laughed as I realized, *"My ship just came in!"*

The next day I shared that story during my keynote and closed with "Writers don't wait for their ship to come in; they write their way out to it." A woman came up afterward and said, "My brother-in-law is the captain of the *San Salvador*. Would you like to meet him?"

Would I?! And that is how I found myself interviewing Captain Ray Ashley below decks on the ship the next day. He told me, "Our first obstacle was cost; the San Diego Maritime Museum estimated it would cost $6.2 million to build the ship, and their entire annual budget was $4.6 million. So, on paper, it didn't make sense to proceed. Fortunately, our community believed in us and approved the project. Thanks to their support we made the pivotal decision to build the ship in *public* instead of in *private*, which directly led to our success."

"How so?"

"We built the ship in plain view right next to a busy freeway by the airport. Within the first few weeks, we had fifty volunteers—from laypeople to skilled craftsmen, shipwrights, architects—offering their services.

"They helped us persevere through one crisis after another. For example, white oak was the only wood dense enough to carry the weight of this ship, so we bought up the entire world's supply. It took months to mill the wood into the curves of the hull. When we applied epoxy to make it waterproof, the wood startling curling and rotting because the epoxy was contaminated. One of our volunteers said, 'You should call this guy I know. He's an expert on live oak.' Sure enough, live oak was compatible and the vendor was able to supply us with enough to meet our needs.

"Then it was time to embed lead into the hull for ballast, but the price had skyrocketed and we couldn't afford it. A volunteer suggested a 'Get the Lead Out' campaign, and people donated their fish weights, ball bearings, etc. We appreciated their help, but we'd never be able to accumulate the amount of lead we needed a few ounces at a time. Once again, our volunteers saved the day. One suggested we get in touch with

a contractor he knew. We tracked him down and explained our situation. The next day he called and asked, 'How much lead do you need?'

"One hundred and eighty thousand pounds."

"The guy chuckled and said, 'Well, I've got one hundred and ninety
thousand pounds of lead and you can have it all.'"

Ray looked at me, "You can't make this stuff up. Those are just a
few of the 'wouldn't believe it if it weren't true' things that happened
while building the ship. Do you know what's even more amazing? Even
though it took three times longer to build the ship than anticipated, it
still came in only a little over its original budget. That is 100 percent
due to all the volunteers who pitched in."

$$1 + 1 = 11$$

"When you can't keep up, connect."

— MARY LOVERDE

What a wonderful example that when we launch our Someday project
in public, we create a rising tide, $1 + 1 = 11$ relationship. People will
leverage their six degrees of separation to remove obstacles, solve problems, and expedite success. They add their cumulative expertise, energy,
and alliances and improve the quality of the experience for everyone
involved.

When I interviewed Captain Ray on the *San Salvador* that day in
Morro Bay, there were lines of people waiting to tour it. Ray said, "We
gave donors and volunteers an opportunity to hammer their initials into
the keel. It's been so rewarding to see them point to the part of the ship
they worked on or funded and say, 'I did that!' They're so proud to be
part of the story, and to be able to put their hands on something they
helped bring into being."

As I wrapped up my time with Ray, I couldn't help but reflect on
the many ways the *San Salvador* project was a metaphor for my Year by
the Water project.

I too launched a venture when the "numbers" weren't there. It was going to cost more money than was in my budget, and I had to trust the funding would show up. I too launched in public and experienced an outpouring of support; e.g., "I have a cabin in Point Reyes National Seashore." "Come visit me in Niagra Falls." I too benefitted from being connected with a community who leveraged their six degrees of separation to make this journey financially feasible and even more meaningful and successful.

Which Side of the FEARS–FAITH Ledger Are You Focusing On?

"Consult not your fears, but your hopes and dreams. Think not about your frustrations, but about your unfulfilled potential."
—POPE JOHN XXIII

How about you? What is the Today, Not Someday project you want to launch? If for some reason you're hesitating, it can help to fill out the Fears–Faith Ledger to see which side you're focusing on. Because whichever side you're focusing on can determine whether you choose to "play it safe" or "play it forward."

Start filling in any doubts or concerns you've been harboring under the Fears column on the left. Maybe this project is going to cost more than you originally planned. Maybe you're heading off into the unknown and there are no guarantees. Maybe a significant other doesn't want you to do this. Be realistic and honest about your fears.

Now, switch over to the right column and focus on your faith that you believe this venture is worth doing. Write down what it would mean to you to bet on yourself and launch this after thinking about it for so long. Write down how you can GTS this and learn along the way. Write how you plan to build your project in public and create a "rising tide raising your ship" community.

FEARS	**FAITH**
_____	_____
_____	_____
_____	_____
_____	_____
_____	_____

Now, look at the two columns. If you stay focused on the left side of the ledger, your project will stay in the boatyard. However, if you switch over to the right side and focus on all its potential benefits, it can give you the confidence and courage to set your creative vision in motion.

When you do launch your dream project, be sure to tell people what you're doing. Share your vision in an announcement to your online network. Ask for ideas. Enlisting help adds an all-important ingredient to the equation. A project that may initially seem daunting or "unrealistic" is now feasible because you won't be operating in isolation and supplying all your own resources. You will be leveraging a group of people who are doing everything in their power to help you move your project forward because they are invested in its success.

And isn't that what we want? Not just a productive life where the light is on in our eyes, but to be able to share what we care about with a community who cares about it too?

Ask For—and Graciously Accept—Help

"Sometimes accepting help is harder than offering it."
—STAR WARS: THE CLONE WARS

J. C. Chamberlain, a marketing executive, is another shining example of what can happen when we ask for and accept help. John was approaching his fiftieth birthday and wanted to do something special. He thought, "I know, I'll set a world record."

"What?!" you ask. Well, that's how J.C. rolls. As a former nationally ranked cyclist and rower, he started researching what record he might have a shot at. He decided he had a chance at the cycling record for amount of distance covered in one hour for his age group. He announced his intentions, complete with a start and goal date, to his friends and Facebook community.

As soon as he did, people started jumping on his bandwagon. One said, "I work with a former Olympic coach. Here's his contact info." Another said, "I have contacts with avelodrome in Southern California," Another said, "Why not sleep in a hyperbaric chamber? It will expedite your oxygen efficiency, and I know where to get one." Another said, "I'm a videographer and I'd like to do a documentary about this."

Notice, these people weren't just cheering him on; they were providing connections that increased his likelihood of his success. And they were also providing accountability. He was no longer just pursuing this dream for himself; he had a team counting on him.

Want the rest of that story? J.C. did go for his world record. He rented use of the track and showed up with his team after a year of intense twice-daily training, nutritional diligence, and all-out dedication. He zoomed onto the track, and knew within a few laps he wasn't going to break the record. Every athlete knows that some days you're at your energetic best. Other days, not so much. As J.C. said afterward, "It was just one of those days."

He had a decision to make. Was he going to give up? Nope, J.C. continued to give *his* best even though he knew it was not going to be *the* best. The sign of a champion.

J.C. said, "Not only do I not regret going for the record, it was one of the most rewarding experiences of my life. I met people I wouldn't have met. Stretched myself in ways I'll always be proud of. Got in the best shape of my life. A pretty good way to celebrate becoming fifty."

One of the many things I love about J.C.'s story was that it shows that even when we don't fulfill our original dream; the quest can still be a success.

Make Your Project Visible to Make It More Viable

"If everyone is moving forward together, success takes care of itself."
— HENRY FORD

Want another way to make your Today, Not Someday project more *viable?* Make it *visible.*

At the end of a writing retreat, a participant named Julie raised her hand and said, "I have loved every minute of this week. My husband is a pilot. This is the writer's version of what he calls 'hangar flying.' Unfortunately, I know what will happen as soon as I get home. Life. A couple weeks from now my plans to write a book will be back on the shelf and all my good intentions will be gone. Any suggestions on how to keep our writing dreams alive?"

I told her, "Draft your book cover and post it where you'll see it every every day. Call your local bookstore and ask if they have a writer's support group. If so, join it. As you said, there's no substitute for hanging with your author peeps and 'book flying.'"

Julie got in touch a few weeks later. "Sam, I followed up on your suggestions to take my project public instead of operating in isolation. I joined a private Facebook authors' group where we post pages online and get feedback, but it's that book cover on the refrigerator that keeps me motivated. Every time I see it, I'm inspired to keep going instead of giving up."

A friend who hosts vision-board parties said, "Sam, I hope you're going to recommend that people get together for a vision-board party. Every single person who has ever attended one of my events says it's surreal how things that didn't make sense at the time end up coming true."

That's not just my friend's experience. A 2016 *Forbes* article by Eilene Zimmerman reported the results of a survey done by TD Bank. As she said, "If you've ever poked fun at someone for creating a vision board as a way to picture success, you may not be laughing after you see the results of a survey done by TD Bank. They found that 82 per cent of small business owners that used a vision board from the get-go reported that they have accomplished more than half the goals they included on that board." This was especially true for millennials who have grown up online using digital images to tell the story of their lives on social platforms like Facebook, Instagram, and YouTube.

Want to increase the likelihood of your dreams coming true? Host a Today, Not Someday vision-board party. Invite friends over. Make a trip to the library to pick up different types of magazines for free (or for a few cents each). Give everyone a stack of magazines, a poster board, glue stick, and some scissors. Play upbeat music. Let the fun begin.

When you're finished, don't put your vision board away where it's out of sight, out of mind. Post it where you'll see it frequently to visually reinforce what you want your upcoming months to look and feel like on a daily basis. Sheryl Sandberg said, "Dream long. Plan short." The more public you make and keep your vision, the more likely it is your dream and plan will happen in the short term and in the long term.

19

Create a Community of One

"The only time we waste is the time we spend thinking we're alone."

—Mitch Albom

had a decision to make. I was sitting at an intersection and could either take the on-ramp to Route 10 or stay on this country road. I was driving from Houston to California for the third time and vowed on the spot, "I am *not* going through El Paso or taking Route 10, ever again." The second I selected the blue highway, the anti-interstate, I knew I'd made the right decision. Whenever I got to a crossroad, I just took whatever road headed *west*.

I had always pictured Texas as hot, dry, and barren. But this was Hill Country in spring. Much to my surprise, everything was alive and full of color. I was driving at my favorite time of day—golden hour, the gentle moments just before the sun goes down and the air calms and shimmers.

I crested a hill and was treated with a golden field stretching out to the horizon and on all sides of me. I was . . . awestruck. I pulled over and shut off the car engine. The only sound was a slight breeze through a nearby tree. Otherwise, it was majestically silent. I was completely immersed in the moment. Blissfully connected. One with everything.

Connected? How could I feel connected? There was no one around.

Well, if there's anything I learned on my Year by the Water, it's that there's all kinds of connection. There was connection to that place, to the magnificence of that moment, and to how grateful I was to be imprinting that extraordinary experience. I was in good company!

Don't You Ever Get Lonely?

"It is only in solitude that I ever find my own core."
— ANNE MORROW LINDBERGH

Are you thinking, "Really?! *Didn't you ever get lonely being by yourself?*" Do you know that was *the* most frequently asked question on my Year by the Water?

My answer was always a resounding *no*. I never felt lonely. I felt . . . connected. Connected to my family and friends who were with me even when they weren't with me. Connected to the warmth of the sun, the feel of the breeze, how fortunate I felt to be alive, free and experiencing this.

You may also be wondering if I ever got bored driving cross-country by myself.

Once again, the answer was an emphatic *no*.

When I was driving for hours (or days) at a time, I never got bored because I listened to books on tape and podcasts. Jonathan Fields's *Good Life Project*. Guy Raz on NPR's *How I Built This*. Ashlee Vance's brilliant biography of Elon Musk. Misty Copeland's *Life in Motion*.

To me, it was the best of all worlds. Discovering new physical territory and new psychological territory. New places. New ideas. Mental and visual engagement and stimulation. Bliss.

It was crystal clear to me. If I ever felt lonely or bored, it meant I wasn't paying attention.

We're Never Really Alone If We Pay Attention

"We need society, and we need solitude also, as we need summer and winter, day and night, exercise and rest."

— PHILIP GILBERT HAMERTON

Are you thinking, "Wait a minute. The last chapter talked about the benefits of a community, and this hack is called AFFILIATE, yet you're talking about preferring to be by yourself?"

The answer to that is *"Not all the time. Some of the time."*

I think many of us don't get enough alone time. We work in cities where we're surrounded by people. We live in apartment buildings with neighbors feet away. We drive on highways with people in front of us, behind us, and on all sides of us. We eat at restaurants, get gas and groceries, go shopping, see movies, and run errands with people all around us.

For many of us, having "space" is an anomaly, a luxury.

For example, I was driving out in the middle of nowhere listening to Gloria Steinem's *My Life on the Road*. Gloria shared Virginia Woolf's insight that "Every woman needs a room of her own." I started laughing as I realized, "I have a *road* of my own."

To me, an open road is the essence of freedom. No committees. No red tape. No one telling me what I can or can't do. Just an open road offering limitless options.

One of the many reasons this was so welcome is that it was the opposite of my norm. For years, my days had been filled with events and appointments. I was often speaking at or attending conferences. Even when I was home, I was usually on the phone with consults, so I was interacting with people, even when I was home "alone."

You Don't Have to Be Anti-Social to Be Pro-Solitude

*"What a lovely surprise to finally discover how unlonely
being alone can be."*

—ELLEN BURSTYN

Some people I met on my travels had a hard time wrapping their head around the fact that I never felt lonely. When the guy at the counter of a barbecue shack heard I was traveling cross-country by myself, he said, "Really?! You don't ever wish you had someone to share things with?"

"Nope. I'm loving every minute just the way it is."

He said, "I don't get that. If I didn't have someone with me, it would feel kind of . . . empty."

I thought about why being alone feels "full" for me instead of "empty." And it brought back what it was like walking into Lincoln's Cottage in Washington, D.C.

I had spent the day training the international board of an entrepreneur organization. They had arranged to host a private dinner at this historical spot where Lincoln rode his horse to get away from the pressures of the White House and write the Emancipation Proclamation.

I got there an hour before the rest of the group so, except for the caterers, I had the place to myself. The first thing I noticed as I walked in was how "spare" it was. Each room had just a few items. A desk. A chair. A table. One picture on the wall. As I looked around at the absence of stuff, it was as if the walls were whispering, *"Space to think. Space to think."*

I instantly got it. *This* was where Lincoln came to be alone with his thoughts. *This* was where he was able to escape the "madding crowd" and find the solitude to create that visionary document that changed the course of our nation. I don't think Lincoln was lonely while working there; I think he welcomed the opportunity to immerse himself in that much-needed isolation.

Lincoln wasn't anti-social; he was pro-solitude. I'm projecting but I believe Lincoln understood the need for, and took responsibility for, creating a *balance* of solitude and socialization.

Many inventors and artists talk about their need for solitude. It is when and where they do their best work. It is when they are alone they are able to dig deep—without distractions or interruptions—and envision innovative ideas or break-through solutions. They don't see solitude as being lonely; they see it as a creative necessity.

Yet in today's rush-rush world, few of us have the time and space to go deep into contemplation and creation. And that can result in a life that feels "crowded." A life that's not our own.

Do You Crave Solitude?

"I have to be alone very often. That's how I refuel."

— AUDREY HEPBURN

How about you? Are you around people all the time? Do you feel "crowded"? Do you yearn for a room, a road, a space of your own?

A mother with three young children told me, "I can't even go to the bathroom without having one of my kids pound on the door, wanting something. When I go grocery shopping and my husband takes care of the kids, I sometimes stop at a park on the way back home to steal a nap or just to do *nothing*."

How will you take responsibility for getting some alone time? It's not being standoffish, it's crucial to your mental and physical well-being. As Audrey Hepburn pointed out, we need a little psychic territory to get away from the pressures of daily life and refuel.

The caveat to this? Many overwhelmed people told me they crave alone time, but some people told me they're afraid to be alone. In fact, a Science.org article by Nadia Whitehead was titled, "People Would Rather Be Electrically Shocked Than Be Alone with Their Thoughts." She shared a study done by University of Virginia in which participants chose to voluntarily shock themselves rather than sit in a room alone with their thoughts and with "nothing to do."

Where are you on this spectrum? Craving quiet time or avoiding it?

Only Connect

"To go out with the setting sun on an empty beach is
to truly embrace your solitude."

—JEANNE MOREAU

Mark, a musician who's considered the life of the party everywhere he goes, told me, "Everyone assumes I'm an extrovert because I'm such a public person. It's true that I come alive and can be 'on' when I'm around people. But if I don't follow it with some private time, I go crazy."

He's not alone. Some people are both extroverts and introverts. There's even a name for this—*ambiverts*.

That was another reason my Year by the Water was so satisfying. It was an exercise in ambivertism. I wasn't around people all the time and I wasn't alone all the time. It was a sublime balance of both. If I'd been solo for a few days and was ready for some company, all I had to do was ask someone at the next table, "What do you suggest I do while I'm in the area?"

The quickest way to turn strangers into friends is to ask for their advice. As Malcolm Forbes used to say, "The way to a man's heart is through his opinion." The way to almost anyone's heart is to ask for their advice. For example, asking "What do you suggest . . ." is the quickest way to bypass superficial chitchat or meaningless small talk.

A participant in one of our Someday Salons pushed back when I told our group how easy it was to connect with people on the road. He said, "Sam, it may be easy for you. But I'm shy. I can't walk up to a total stranger and strike up a conversation."

I told him, "Yes, you can. I think labeling ourselves as 'shy' becomes an excuse for not approaching people. It might be helpful to understand that most people feel uncomfortable in the first few minutes of meeting someone. Even famous people admit to feeling butterflies when walking into a room full of strangers. The key to is decide you're not going to let a label keep you from leading a full and satisfying life."

"But how? How do you overcome shyness?"

"Do what my son Andrew did. When we moved from Maui to the Mainland, he realized it was a chance for a fresh start. No one knew him at this new school so he could be anyone he wanted to be. He just made up his mind that instead of self-labeling himself as shy or socially awkward he was going to be the guy who could talk to girls."

"He got over his nerves just like that?"

"He still felt nervous. The thing was, he knew that girls wanted boys to talk to them. But boys were standing around too afraid to approach the girls because they didn't know what to say and didn't want to look uncool. Somebody had to get things going. He figured it might as well be him. Andrew overcame his initial nervousness and got good at kick-starting conversations. Now, he speaks for companies like Google, Zappos, MasterCard and teaches people what he calls SOCIAL FLOW. As he says, 'A new friend is a smile and a good question away.'"

You may relate to what author Elizabeth Gilbert said, "I am far more of a loner than people would imagine. But I am the most gregarious and socially interactive loner you ever met. The thing is, I am fascinated by people's stories."

How about you? Would you call yourself an introvert, extrovert, or ambivert? Do you, like Andrew, call yourself shy, but now realize you can overcome self-consciousness by asking good questions? Do you, like Elizabeth, enjoy being a loner but understand you can connect with anyone, anytime, anywhere, if you're fascinated by their stories?

Whatever your answers to the above questions, it's important to know where you are on the Solitude–Socialization Continuum. Yes, just like the Serve Others–Serve Ourselves Continuum, it's helpful to have a way to visualize this issue instead of just having fears swirling around in our head.

Remember my friend Lee in chapter 12 who wondered why she felt so burned out and then realized she'd been out twelve nights in a row? She instituted some boundaries around how many evening functions she would agree to so that wouldn't happen again.

And remember that mother of three kids who talked about stopping at a park on the way home from a grocery store to "steal" a nap?

That was nothing to feel guilty about. That was taking responsibility for her alone time.

If you're wondering how, with all your responsibilities, you can carve out time and space for creative solitude, you'll learn how poet W. S. Merwin did that (and you can too) in chapter 23.

LIFE HACK 7

INTEGRATE Your Passion and Profession

"Working hard for something you don't care about is called stress. Working hard for something you love is called passion."

— SIMON SINEK

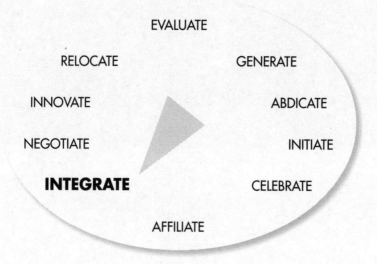

As discussed in previous chapters, some people silo their passion and profession. This section introduces Life Hack 7, which shows how to INTEGRATE your work and recreation instead of seeing them as separate. You'll also discover how to create an encore career where you get paid to do what you're good at so you have the best of both worlds.

20

Blend Your Work and Recreation

"Where the needs of the world and your talents cross,
there lies your vocation."

— Aristotle

My tennis buddy Kathy, a realtor, told me, "Sam, I won't be available to play tennis anymore. With the economy being what it is, I've got to buckle down and concentrate on biz dev."

I told her, "Kathy, there are two luxury hotels right down the street. Why not go to the concierges, let them know you're a 4.5 player, and volunteer to play with resort guests who are looking for a good match? You're active in the Chamber of Commerce and a longtime resident so they can trust you to act with integrity and treat their guests with respect so it will be a win for all involved."

Kathy followed up, and a month later she was back to playing a couple times a week, but this time with visitors who were potential clients. She wasn't inappropriate about it. It was just natural that after a well-played match, the visitors would be curious about what she did for a living. When they discovered she was a realtor, they often wanted to know if there were any good properties for sale, and the conversation would evolve from there.

What I love about Kathy's story is it shows that playing tennis wasn't an indulgence that took time away from Kathy's business; it *was* a way to cultivate new clients and business. The fact that these visitors were staying at a five-diamond hotel prequalified them as having sufficient income to afford the real estate properties in the area. Instead of sitting inside at a desk "cold-calling" people or placing expensive ads in visitor publications, Kathy was staying fit and doing a hobby she loved with people who often became friends and clients. The best of all worlds.

Leverage What You Love

"It is a luxury to combine our passion with our contribution."
— SHERYL SANDBERG

How about you? Do you see your work and recreation as separate? Do they have to be?

The reason I'm bringing this up is because so many people on my travels saw my Year by the Water as a "vacation." I would explain that, yes, it was a vacation, a *working* vacation.

Why do I make this distinction? Because I think the current model of retirement is broken. The whole idea of "waiting" until we're sixty-five or older to do what we want is absurd. I understand this model was centered around our need to accrue savings and social security benefits to finance our "senior" years.

The thing is, by the time we retire, many of us don't have the health or freedom to do the things we've been waiting for *decades* to do. I started this book with the story of my dad who postponed his dream of touring the country to visit the National Parks. I heard *dozens* of variations of that story during my travels.

I stayed at a friend's marvelous home overlooking the Pacific Ocean while wrapping up this manuscript. After a couple of gray rainy days, the sun came out. That was a signal it was time to get up, get outside, and get moving. I was walking through the Seacliff State Park campground when two women popped out of their RV and asked, "Will you take a picture of us?"

"Sure, I will, but you've got to tell me your story."

Turns out Sheila and June were close friends and neighbors. Sheila had looked at June the day before and said, "It's time to take a break."

June resisted and said, "It's going to be your son's birthday next week. You've got to get things ready."

Sheila persisted. She was even wearing a sweatshirt that read: NEVERTHELESS, SHE PERSISTED. She said, "If we don't go now, it'll be months before we can get away."

Nuff said. They told their families they'd be back on Sunday and headed to the beach. I asked, "What gave you such clarity about not waiting for a less busy time?"

Sheila said, "I'm an insurance agent. One of my older clients waited to his late sixties to retire and buy the huge, fancy Winnebago of his dreams. He drove it to my office to show it to me and so I could add it to his account. It took him about twenty minutes to park the darn thing and get out of it because he doesn't move very well. He came in, slammed the door, plopped down and said, 'I waited too damn long, and now I'm too old to enjoy it.' I'll never forget that."

June chimed in, "We've taken our kids everywhere, Hawaii, Disneyland, the Grand Canyon." She said, only half-joking, "We want to make memories with them before they don't want to spend time with us."

I asked if I could share their story because they're such inspiring examples of why not to wait. Later may be too late.

What about you? It's not too late to reverse a penchant for workaholism. Don't be like the gentleman with the RV who waited too long. You don't need an RV and you don't need to take time *off* work. There are ways to combine what you love *with your* work now . . . not someday.

Can You Combine Your Avocation and Your Vocation?

*"The world was shocked to learn I wrote a bestseller at sixty-six.
No matter how long you live, you have stories to tell. What else is there
to do but head off on the Conestoga wagon of the soul?"*

—FRANK MCCOURT

I love the above quote by author Frank McCourt, because his backstory gave so much hope to our Maui Writers Conference attendees. Frank was a high-school English teacher most of his life. It paid the bills and gave him an opportunity to share his love of language with students. But when not at school, he worked on his memoir *Angela's Ashes*, which won the Pulitzer Prize. Frank was a shining example of how your avocation and vocation don't have to be mutually exclusive, you can set off on the Conestoga wagon of your soul and do them *simultaneously*.

Want another example of how to combine your vocation and avocation? I was hired by Nationwide Insurance to present a workshop on how to proactively manage our own career success. Following the program, the event photographer walked up to me and said, "You just described *me*."

"How so?"

"I've worked here in the IT department for years. Up until a couple years ago, I pretty much did my job, but that was it. Came in at nine, left at five. Wasn't very sociable. Then, a coworker found out I was a photographer in my spare time and asked if I'd shoot a fashion show the Women's Network was hosting. The pictures turned out well and word got around. Next thing I knew, people from different departments were asking me to shoot their award luncheons. That led to me being the photographer for the Leadership Series."

"Sound like this has turned into your own private Cheers bar. Everyone knows your name."

"All I know is that I look forward coming into work because every week is different."

More proof of how a hobby can be integrated into a job in a way that adds value for all involved.

So, what do you love to do? Reading? How about hosting a book club for your office colleagues? Community service? Maybe you can lead a corporate team to clean up a local park or playground? Want to get back in shape? Maybe you can host a walking club at lunchtime?

How Can You Make Your Job More Fulfilling?

"Oh, so you hate your job? . . . There's a support group for that. It's called 'Everybody' and they meet in the bar."

— DREW CAREY

Are you thinking, "Sam, I already spend forty hours at work. Why should I expend any more time and effort at a job when I won't get paid extra for it?"

I'm glad you brought that up. While writing this book, I heard dismaying stories and uncovered some rather depressing research about how unhappy people are at work.

There are hundreds of "jokes" and social memes expressing how much people hate their job. Everything from "Sorry I was late. I was sitting in the parking lot not wanting to come in" to "I haven't gone to bed yet and I'm already looking forward to coming home from work tomorrow."

What's the point? We spend a third or more of our life at work. It is *not* a joke to be unhappy for a third or more of our life. It is *not* okay to simply accept that work sucks or hope it will get better . . . someday. Hope is not a strategy.

A better strategy is to take responsibility for making your job more fulfilling. This is not the impossible dream. A family friend who was a colonel at Hickam Air Force Base was able to parlay his golf skills into rounds with visiting dignitaries. Mike's "real job" was in the security department, but news got around he was a scratch golfer. At that time, it was common for statesmen (and women) from other countries to come to Hawaii for Pacific Rim conferences. In their off time, some liked to hit the links at Hickam or Schofield Barracks. They needed a decent player with a security clearance, so Mike got the call. He had experiences he never would have had, all because he was long off the tee and had a killer short game.

How about you? Are you an excellent athlete? Chances are your corporate VIPs and clients would enjoy connecting with an athlete they can trust to give them a good match.

I'm speaking from experience. I had the privilege of working with Rod Laver at his tennis resort on Hilton Head Island. I was not a pro but had a decent game. As a result, I got to play with celebrities who were vacationing on Hilton Head. Then, I was recruited to open a country club for racquet sports near Washington, D.C., where I met captains of industry and got to play at the White House. Never would have happened if I hadn't been able to get the ball back over the net.

And if you're thinking, "I don't play sports and I don't have any special skills I can parlay into enjoying my job," check out the Purpose Prize award-winners at Encore.org. You'll discover innovative ways "everyday" people have created enterprises that are positively impacting all involved.

Create More Meaningful Work

"It is good to have an end to journey toward;
but it is the journey that matters, in the end."

—URSULA LEGUIN

Would you like your work to be your play and your play to be your work?

Keep in mind what Natalie Goldberg says, "Writers live twice." I think authors and artists get to live life thrice. We experience something in the moment. We experience it again when we write it, paint it, film it, or snap a picture of it. And we experience it again when we share it with others and hear how it impacted them.

Please understand, you don't have to be a professional to share your work online, whether it's posting your travel photos on Facebook, blogging your business insights on LinkedIn, displaying your art projects on Instagram, or sharing cooking videos on YouTube.

If you visit interesting places, meet interesting people, do interesting things, chances are people will want to see it, hear about it, or read about it. In the next chapter I'll share specific ways you can get paid to do this. The question for now is: What is your passion? Your purpose? How can you combine them into a meaningful profession so you're enjoying the journey?

Do You Have a Cause That Is Calling You?

"I've never seen a separation between work and play. It's all living."
— Richard Branson

We've been talking about how to combine your passion and profession so your career contributes to your quality of life.

Want another way to do meaningful work now, not later? Think about a cause that is calling you, an issue that needs addressing, a problem that needs solving. Dedicating yourself to that can give your life meaning and purpose and help create a lasting legacy.

You may be thinking, "I'm a little young to be thinking about legacy. Isn't that something we do in the last years of our life?"

Well, no. Legacy is simply leading a life that will make an enduring positive difference for others. We can do that at any age. Cassandra Lin is a shining example.

I attended an annual innovation conference in Rhode Island called BIF. Keynoters featured Tony Hsieh of Zappos, and other leading-edge thinkers who are creating solutions to some of the world's most pressing problems.

However, the most impressive person was the one who came out, stood tall, and waited until the room was quiet. She then leaned in to the group and said with a twinkle in her eye, "I know what you're thinking, 'What's a thirteen-year old got to teach me about innovation?'"

The audience laughed (she had read their mind!) and she continued to tell her story. She and her seventh-grade class had gone on a field trip into the sewers of Providence. Their guide told them the sewers were filled with FOG (Fat, Oil, and Grease), a disaster waiting to happen. Cassandra thought, "Someone should do something about this." Then she thought, "That somebody could be me. I will do something about this."

So, she founded TGIF—Thank God It's Fuel. Every Saturday, she and her classmates visit the restaurants in the area and in the industrial parks and collect the FOG. They then take it to a processing plant where it's turned into fuel. They donate the money they receive from this to families who can't afford to heat their homes in winter.

Cassandra Lin is not waiting for her later years to leave a legacy. Her life has meaning and purpose now. She's not waiting for someday or for someone. She is the change she wishes to see.

Look around. Do you see something "wrong"? Do you think, "Somebody should *do* something about this?" Remember, *you're* as much a somebody as anybody. Maybe *you* can do something about it.

C. S. Lewis said, "You can't go back and change the beginning, but you can start where you are and change the ending." How will you stop waiting for rewarding work to come to you and start meeting it in the middle? How can you blend a cause and your career to change *the* world and change *your* world? What will you start this week to make your job more enjoyable?

21

Don't Wait for Work You Love; Create Work You Love

"The only way to do great work is to love what you do.
If you haven't found it yet, keep looking."

— STEVE JOBS

A forty-something woman named Val said, "I hope you know how lucky you are to earn a living doing work you love. Not everyone can do that. Some of us have to have 'regular jobs.'"

I agreed, "You're right. We do need people to do regular jobs. We need people to work in our factories, farms, and in food service. That is the reality for many people and they deserve props for being responsible and doing what it takes to put food on the table. The point is, if you're doing work that drains you, are there hacks that could make it more meaningful instead of just resigning yourself to the fact that you dread going into work every day?"

"That sounds kind of Pollyanna-ish to me."

"I understand. All we're doing here is exploring options instead of simply sitting back and accepting our fate. One way to do that is to look at what you do in your free time. Noticing what you do when you're *not* working can reveal career options you might not have considered."

For example, Dana Wasson always used to "noodle and doodle" in class. Even in college, she always had a pen in her hand and was sketching or drawing on any piece of paper that was handy. Unfortunately, since her doodling and daydreaming had been framed as a problem, ("Get your head out of the clouds,") she initially didn't think it could be turned into a career. After pursuing other jobs though, she finally realized she could earn a *good* living (in every sense of the word) doing what she loved.

Dana is a visual facilitator, the person you see at conferences listening to the discussion and drawing it into a colorful word-map. She literally and figuratively gets everyone on the same page with her meeting-mural art that captures the conversation in a colorful keepsake. Dana turned her joy into her job. Isn't it worth exploring if you might be able to do the same?

Leverage Your Four I's to Create a Career Calling

"Finding your passion isn't just about careers and money. It's about finding your authentic self. The one you've buried beneath other people's needs."

— KRISTEN HANNAH

A key to doing work you love is to stop thinking you will *find* it, as if it exists out there intact and all you have to do is look long enough and *eureka!*—there it will be, hiding behind a tree. Work we love more often *emerges* from doing what we're good at. It is a result of *acting on* what calls us and *creating* a career path that is congruent with what we care about.

You may be thinking, "Sounds good in theory, but *how* do I do this in practice?"

Well, here's how I created my career as an Authorpreneur. I didn't even know this profession existed when I was growing up. There was no degree in this at college. No newspaper ads with job announcements hiring for this type of work. No map to follow. No directions.

The work I'm doing is the result of *intuitive* yet strategic steps I took along the way that honored what I call the Four I's of our Career Compass. When I had career decisions to make and didn't know what to do, I checked in with my Instincts, Interests, Integrity, Initiative.

Invariably, the Four I's pointed me in the right direction and provided my next step. Honoring my Career Compass has yielded a truly satisfying success that feels right in my heart.

It started back when I needed to make my first major career decision: choosing my college major. Thanks to my dad giving me W. H. Murray's inspiring quote (page 78 in chapter 3) and encouraging me to bet on my gut, I had the prescience to honor my Four I's.

INSTINCTS: My instincts were telling me to take the unconventional path of studying R.A. instead of following the advice to become a doctor or lawyer.

INTERESTS: I loved playing, coaching, and organizing sports so studying Recreation Administration was in alignment with my interests.

INTEGRITY: Money was not my primary motivator, doing something that mattered and that would make a positive difference for people was my True Priority.

INITIATIVE: I didn't wait for job opportunities to come my way. I actively pitched myself into professional opportunities that were in alignment with my three other I's.

A student named Mark said, "I get the Four I's, but how did that lead to your current career?"

"Years ago, I was reading *The Washington Post* and noticed the word 'concentration' was used six times in the sports section. Tennis player Chris Evert said her ability to stay focused despite the planes flying overhead was why she'd been able to win the U.S. Open. A golfer

who missed a putt on a sudden-death playoff hole said he'd lost his focus because he was distracted by the clicking cameras of nearby photog-
raphers. I was intrigued. (I've since come to understand that when
we're intrigued, opportunity is knocking on our heart.)"

I thought, "We all wish we could concentrate better but no one ever
teaches us how. It is the key to success in just about everything but I've
never seen any books on this subject. And it *matters*."

"This topic *interested* me. I felt it would benefit people so it was
aligned with my *integrity*. My *instincts* were telling me there was a commercial need for this and people would pay to be taught how to do it
better. I decided to *initiate* a deep dive into the topic with the goal of
offering public workshops. Instead of reading other people's work, I created a ten-question W Quiz to kick-start anecdotal research. I interviewed 'everyday people' to glean their insights."

Develop a W Quiz to Create Your Own Unique Body of Work

"The most important thing is not to stop questioning."

— ALBERT EINSTEIN

Here is the W quiz I used to develop my methodology. Feel free to adapt
this to a topic you would like to teach or a talent you think people would
like to have, whether that's making craft beer or raising confident kids.
Just substitute your subject where I use the word "concentrate."

1. **What** does concentration mean to you? How would you define it?
2. **Who** modeled or taught concentration to you? What did
   they say/do that had lasting impact?
3. **Who** is an example of someone who *can't* concentrate? Why are
   they not good at it?
4. **When and Where** is a time you concentrated well? What fa-
   cilitated that state of focus/flow?

5. **When** is a time you didn't concentrate well? What blocked or prevented your focus/flow?
6. **Why** is concentration so important? What are the benefits, the advantages, of doing it well?
7. **What** is your best advice on how to concentrate? What best practice would you like to share?
8. **Who** else should I interview about this topic? **Who** might be a good resource with good tips?

Based on the answers to this W Quiz (and my own experiences), I developed a step-by-step approach on how to concentrate—no matter what—and offered it for Open University. Several participants came up afterward and said, "Will you speak at our conference or teach our employees how to do this?" That one workshop launched a rewarding career that has taken me around the world and given me opportunities to work with the U.S. Embassy in London, Capital One, National Geographic, and Intel. It even resulted in a book titled *Conzentrate*.

After I'd explained this to Mark, he said, "Okay, I got how this kick-started your career. By why the quiz?"

"The goal is to develop *your own* intellectual capital. Instead of reading all the experts' books and cutting-and-pasting their intellectual property into your work, it's important to bring your own original experience, expertise, and epiphanies to the table and create your own body of work.

"'Street interviews' with everyday people help you create a *unique* body of work. Interview everyone. Taxi drivers. Waiters. Attorneys, artists, entrepreneurs. People love being asked for their stories. It immerses you in your subject and guarantees you are addressing current needs, featuring different voices, and offering real-life insights that work.

"You can create a business wrapped around what *you* know that *other people* want to know. People will gladly pay for your methodology because you're expediting their path to get better at something they care about. If you provide people a shortcut to their success, you'll never have to 'work' another day in your life because you'll be making money and making a difference. And isn't that what we all want?"

Build an Encore Career Around What You're Good At

"The very least you can do in your life is to figure out what you hope for . . . and the most you can do is live inside that hope."

— BARBARA KINGSOLVER

Want an example of how to do this? Woody and Eleanor Ruff were retired teachers who wanted to write a book about everything their students wished their parents knew. We came up with a perfect title: *Long Days, Short Years*. Eleanor called to say they'd been asked to speak on a cruise but were going to turn it down because their manuscript was on a tight deadline.

I said, "Don't cancel the cruise! There will be hundreds of parents and grandparents on board. It's a perfect opportunity to interview people from all walks of life. Just take your version of the W quiz and connect with people at meals and while walking the decks."

They got back in touch to say, "We were the hit of the ship! Everyone wanted to share their advice about what they were glad they did and what they wish they had done differently."

So, what are you good at that other people would like to get good at? Maybe people tell you how much they love your iPhone photos and ask, "How do you take such great pictures?" That's what happened to Lynette Sheppard. People kept complimenting her digital photos so she created an online and in-person workshop sharing her process with others.

That's what happened to endurance athletes Carol Brooks and Lesley Smith. I met them when they handed me a business flyer while I was walking my dog. I was curious about their backstory. They told me their busy careers used to prevent them from putting in the long training hours needed for their triathlons. They would go for long runs on the C&O Canal on weekends, but that wasn't enough for them or for their active dog who was housebound during the day.

Then, their entrepreneurial lightbulb switched on. They realized they weren't the only ones with hyper dogs that were cooped up all day. What if they started a business that offered dog-*running*, not just dog-*walking*? They could take pooches along on their training runs and get paid to do what they wanted to do while giving dog-owners something they wanted done.

I brainstormed a tagline for their startup on the spot—"DogOnFitness: More than a walk around the block." I just visited their website and was delighted to discover they now have locations around Virginia, Maryland, and Delaware. Kudos to them for creating a business that integrated their interests, instincts, integrity, and initiative.

Create Purpose in Your Life by Being Generative

> "I have the world's best job. I get paid to hang out in
> my imagination all day."
>
> —STEPHEN KING

Are you thinking, "Well, good for you, Lynette, Carol, and Lesley. But I don't want to be a speaker, author, coach, or entrepreneur, so those ideas don't help me."

Got it. The *premise of this book is that someday is the busiest day of the week.* Whether we're working, in school, or retired, it's important to have *something* in our life *right now* that gives meaning and momentum to our days. Being *generative* is a nonnegotiable requirement for a satisfying life. The six questions below can help you hone in on what that might be for you—whether you're twenty-two or seventy-two.

1. What hobbies did I have growing up that I really enjoyed but don't do anymore?
2. What do people tell me I'm good at? (Please note: This may come naturally to you so you conclude it's "no big deal." But the very fact this comes easily to you is an indicator it's one of your strengths.

If people consistently compliment you on something, trust their input! What is a talent or knack you have? Making gluten-free snacks? Collecting vintage clothes? Fixing computers?)

3. Who in business do I admire? Do I look at their career and think, "I wish I could do that"?

4. Where can I expedite people's success, wealth, health, or happiness? How can I *save* them time and money, or *make* them time and money?

5. What don't people like to do that I actually like doing?

6. What do I find unacceptable? What do I look at and think, "Someday I should do something about that. I'm as much a somebody as anybody—I'll do something about that"?

Answering these questions can help clarify a special talent, ability, or knack you have that could be at the intersection of your Interests, Instincts, Integrity, and Initiative.

Are You Gifting Your Gifts?

"The meaning of life is to find your gift.
The purpose of life is to give it away."

—PABLO PICASSO

You know how I came up with the questions above? By going to farmers' markets and craft fairs. Whenever I saw one on my travels, I made time to stop and explore, because they are full of *the best* Today, Not Someday stories.

For example, I pulled into my hotel on the Savannah Harbor and discovered the Springtime Made in the South craft show was being held next door at the convention center. Can you say serendipity?

My first stop of the more than two hundred vendors was Lisa Schalk of Toffee to Go. A former stay-at-home mom, she started making homemade white chocolate/macadamia nut toffee from a family recipe for Christmas presents. Recipients begged her to make more.

Her innovative flavors got such raves, she started going to weekend arts/crafts fairs where her delicious, one-of-a-kind toffee kept selling out. She told her husband, Jim, a hospitality executive, "I think we've really got something here."

Jim told me, "I've got to confess. When she told me about this, I thought people were just being 'nice,' and then I went to a festival and witnessed for myself the enthusiastic response. People had been following her online and had driven from hours away to buy her toffee in person. I quit my job and we went all-in full time."

Fast forward. They just bought a 16,000-foot warehouse, have been featured in *O* magazine's Christmas issue, and they ship bulk orders to corporate clients around the country. Lisa told me, "People tell us, 'Oh, you're so lucky that *Oprah's Favorite Things* found you.'" She smiled and said, "Luck is a lot of two a.m. nights, but it's worth it."

I discovered the "Pretty Darn Good Salsa" couple in the next aisle. They created their own special blend with beans, corn, cilantro, and secret ingredients for a Super Bowl party. Everyone loved it. They started making bigger and bigger batches. After retiring (he was a school teacher for decades), they started to hit the road every weekend. He says, "It may be eight degrees back home, but we know we'll be in Florida that Friday to Sunday visiting our daughter and meeting all kinds of interesting people and hearing their stories, while paying for our retirement."

Next I was drawn to a booth featuring wearable art. The proprietor Lynn Shore, told me, "My grandmother, who had the patience of Job, taught me to knit when I was eight. I started handcrafting necklace-scarfs for friends and realized this isn't just a *hobby*, it's a *business*. I used to go to forty-two festivals a year, but I've scaled down." I asked what she liked best about them. She said, eyes bright, "I am inspired by the creativity of humanity. It's a blessing to be here."

What are the morals of these stories? *None* of these business owners studied these careers at college. None of them knew at the time that their passion would end up being a profitable profession. However, all of them are grateful for the blessing of doing work they enjoy that puts the light on in their eyes and the bucks in their bank account.

And yes, I did buy some salsa, toffee, and a scarf while there. Support Small Business!

Could What You Do in Your Free Time Become What You Do Full Time?

"Happiness lies in the joy of achievement and
the thrill of creative effort."

—Franklin D. Roosevelt

Next time you see a craft fair, art show, or farmers market, go! It is an incredible source of inspiration if you ask the proprietors for their "backstories." Chances are they leveraged their Four I's for a creative effort, which has brought them the joy of achievement. Or, as a punny friend calls it, "They turned their hobby into a jobby."

By the way, I agree with Picasso that it's important to gift our gifts. However, I don't agree we should *give them away*. If we need to earn a living, we need to *get paid* for our gifts. Please understand, charging for the value you offer *to* others and add *for* others is 100 percent in integrity. It is fair to generate income when you *do something for* others or *teach something to* others they don't want to do or can't do for themselves.

Remember, it's never too late to create a more rewarding career. John Barrymore said, "A man does not become old until regrets take the place of dreams." Please don't let take regrets replace your dreams. Start thinking *now* how you can navigate the Four I's of your Career Compass to create or integrate a more rewarding life-work.

LIFE HACK 8

NEGOTIATE for What You Want, Need, and Deserve

"The moment you settle for less than you deserve, you get less than you even settled for."

— Maureen Dowd

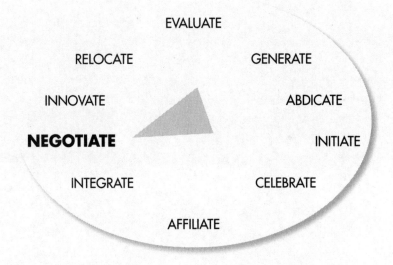

EVALUATE

RELOCATE   GENERATE

INNOVATE   ABDICATE

NEGOTIATE   INITIATE

INTEGRATE   CELEBRATE

AFFILIATE

Life Hack 8 suggests win-win ways to advocate for yourself and speak up for your rights so your personal and professional relationships are more of what you want them to be. You'll also discover how, instead of waiting for things to come your way or go your way, to be proactive and quit watering dead plants and stop ordering pasta you don't want.

22

Stop Trying to Make People Happy; You're Not Chocolate

"You are not required to set yourself on fire to keep other people warm."

—ANONYMOUS

While in NYC for a conference, I met my son Andrew for dinner. I'd been eating healthier so Andrew made a reservation for one of the area's top-rated vegan restaurants. Andrew texted he was running late and suggested I go ahead and order. I scanned the menu. Nothing looked even vaguely appetizing. It was succotash here, tofu there, broccoli everywhere.

I understood this place was a goldmine for veggie-lovers. However, not too long ago, I ran the other direction at the first sight of peas and their brethren.

Then, I discovered, much to my amazement, you could blend spinach and kale into a green juice and it actually tasted good and was good for you. Who knew?! This was a mini-miracle after years of avoiding vegetables. It changed my diet, body, energy, and life.

Back to the restaurant. The only thing I saw on the menu I thought I could get down was linguine with clam sauce, so I ordered that for me and the special for Andrew.

Andrew arrived moments later on his ever-present skateboard. He took one look at my steaming pile of linguine and said, "Mom, I thought you weren't eating pasta."

"I'm not."

Double-take. Andrew looked at me, looked at the pasta. "Then why did you order the pasta?"

"Andrew, it's no big deal."

He looked at me in consternation. "Mom, it is a big deal. You say you're not eating pasta, but you just ordered pasta. I don't get it."

I tried to brush this aside so we could focus on getting caught up. "Andrew, let's just have our meal. We only have a couple hours before I need to catch the train."

Andrew persisted, "Mom, why did you order something you didn't want?"

I could see he wasn't going to let this go (good for him) so I tried to explain my thought process. "Andrew, I didn't see anything on the menu I wanted, and we only have a little time, so I ordered the only thing I thought I could eat."

"Mom, do you know what a mixed message that sends?"

Wow. I never thought of it that way. I realized, in that moment, I'd been "ordering pasta I didn't want" for decades. My default was to read people's mind, anticipate what they might want, and give it to them in the hopes of making them happy. I did this with what I thought were good intentions. I didn't want to hurt Andrew's feelings so I was going to down the pasta because I didn't want to make an issue of it.

What I didn't realize? I *was* making an issue of it. Instead of telling the truth, I was creating confusion and an underlying feeling of dissonance. Thank heaven Andrew got to the heart of the matter. "Mom, what do you want to eat?"

This time, I told him straight out, "A steak."

He said, "We can do that." He asked our waiter to package up our meals and we walked to Whole Foods, a block away. I bought some hangar steak. He got a salad. We walked to a nearby park and sat outside under a full moon, each of us enjoying what we wanted in the first place . . . connection.

Andrew was curious, "Mom, I still don't understand. Why do you do that?"

"Andrew, I never wanted to be high-maintenance. I grew up deferring to what I thought others wanted in a misguided attempt to avoid conflict. You're showing me that even when I do this with the best of intentions, it produces the exact opposite of what I want. It's *cleaner* and *clearer* to just say outright what I want at the beginning."

"Exactly. When you say what you want, I don't have to read between the lines."

"I get that. The irony is, when you and Tom were growing up, we agreed to tell each other the truth because it makes life so much simpler. We agreed that back-and-forth, 'What movie do you want to see?' 'I don't care, what movie do *you* want to see?' is crazy-making. We promised to talk straight because we agreed that was better than having to second-guess everything and wonder if there's a hidden agenda somewhere."

Andrew just looked at me as if this ought to be a BAOTO— Blinding Attack Of The Obvious. It was crystal clear to him how much simpler it is just to ask for what we want—the first time. It's taking me awhile to undo decades of "chocolate-like" attempts to make everyone happy.

Does any of this sound familiar? Do you "read minds" and do what you think will make people happy? Is it possible that the people in your life would prefer you to tell your truth instead of tip-toeing around it?

Is Your Motto "Is Everybody Happy?"

"My happiness depends on me, so you're off the hook."

—ESTHER HICKS

Now, you might think I got clarity around this, but no. Seems lifelong habits take awhile to undo. Later than year, I met up with Tom, Patty, their son Mateo, and daughter Natalia in Maui for Christmas vacation. What a satisfying full-circle experience it was revisiting Wailea Beach, where Tom and his brother Andrew grew up, and greeting Santa (in aloha attire) paddling up to the beach in an lei-covered outrigger canoe . . . just like he did thirty years ago.

We drove to Black Rock in Kaanapali on our final day, one of the islands' top snorkeling spots. Tom and Patty asked, "Will you watch the kids while we go in?"

"Happy to." Mateo took a little nap and Natalia played contentedly in the sand while I watched Tom and Patty cavort like honeymooners. When they came out of the ocean and started toweling off, Patty asked, "How are you?"

"Oh, we had the best time. Mateo has been in la-la land, and Natalia found this bucket and . . ."

Patty gave me a funny look and said, "No, Sam, I asked how *you* are . . ."

Busted. I guess many of us parents have grown so accustomed to focusing on our kids, when we're asked how *we* are, we automatically give a state of union address about how *they* are. Their welfare is so front and center in our mind that we don't factor ourselves into the picture.

It's time to put ourselves back in the picture. And I mean that literally and figuratively.

Remember in chapter 7 (see page 61) when I talked about my friend Mary helping me "clean house"? While having breakfast, she went to get some eggs out of the fridge and stopped short. She studied the refrigerator door for a moment and then beckoned me over. "Notice anything?"

I went over and studied the pictures. Pictures of Tom and Andrew surfing in Maui. Pictures of them playing Little League. With friends on school field trips At the prom. Graduating.

Guess what wasn't on the refrigerator? Pictures of me. Oh, there were a few family photos, but none of me speaking, on book tours, or with my friends. My refrigerator was telling quite a story . . . and *I wasn't in it.*

The double irony? Even though my sons were grown and out on their own, they were still the primary residents of my home. I had taken myself out of the picture of my own life.

How about you? Have you taken yourself out of the picture of your own life? Do you continue to put other people front and center in your life and home—even when they are out on their own? Isn't it time to put yourself in the picture . . . literally and figuratively?

Are You Too Nice for Your Own Good?

"People can't walk all over you unless you lie down."

— Ann Landers

There's another unintended consequence of being a habitual people-pleaser. For many of us, it has been so long since we've asked for what we want, we no longer know what that is. After burying our needs and wishes for years, they're off our radar. We've sublimated ourselves so often, we just immediately acquiesce so we're not a "bother."

We even waive what we want when no one is around. Remember my Pacific Coast Highway experience, "No, *you* go first." I was lucky that experience didn't cost me my life.

One of the most rewarding aspects of presenting workshops on this topic is when people get in touch to tell me that little Four-Minute–Four-Box Happiness Quiz motivated them to put themselves back in their own story.

Tara said, "I didn't share my answers with anyone that night because I wasn't ready to talk about it in a room full of people. In Box 2 (What

I was *not doing* that I wanted to do) was break up with my fiancé. In Box 3 (what I was doing that I *didn't want to do*), was be engaged to him.

"On paper, we appear to be a good match. We're both in an orchestra and give music lessons to supplement our income. After just a few dates, he proposed. My parents were so happy I'd found someone. He's a nice guy but—and I know this sounds mean—I'm simply not attracted to him. I can't imagine spending the rest of our lives together and it's all he talks about.

"After hearing your 'pasta' story and filling out that box, my gut was saying loud and clear. '*I do not want to marry this man.*' Yet, I put off breaking up with him because I didn't want to hurt his feelings. I know how ridiculous that sounds. I can't believe I went along with this for so long because I didn't know how to end it. It may seem silly, but that little quiz gave me the courage to tell my truth. I rehearsed over and over in my mind what to say, and then I told him as simply as I could. I can hardly express the relief I feel to be, well, there's no other word for it . . . free."

Tara is right. How often do we dodge issues because we don't want to hurt people's feelings? Contrary to what we may have been taught, trying to make other people happy makes no one happy. I'm not suggesting we think only of what we want. I'm suggesting we maintain a better balance between honoring what others want and what we want. Remember what the college counselor said about setting boundaries? "What example am I setting when I honor other people's wishes and not my own? What am I modeling when I take myself out of the story?"

Next time you're about to say yes when your gut is saying no, ask yourself, "Am I ordering pasta I don't want?"

Your future depends on many things, mostly on you. If you want to be happier now, not someday, stop tiptoeing around the truth. Say how you really feel and ask for what you really want . . . from the beginning. It is so much cleaner. People no longer have to read your mind and you no longer have to read theirs. As Mary J. Blige would say, "No more drama."

Want some specific ways to *ask* for what you want and *get* it? Keep reading.

23

If You Don't Ask,
The Answer's Always No

"Argue for your limitations, and sure enough, they're yours."

—RICHARD BACH

As I drove up Connecticut Avenue in Washington, D.C., and past the former Open University offices, I thought back to a pivotal experience that taught me a lot about not waiting for people to give us what we think we deserve.

I had left the tennis industry after realizing that as much as I enjoyed it, I did not want the rest of my life to consist of selling tennis warm-ups, booking courts, and putting on tournaments. So, I took off across Canada in a green Econoline van with a friend to figure out my *Next*. We ran in hayfields that stretched out as far as we could see under the Saskatchewan sun, worked at the Calgary Stampede, and hiked in the magnificent mountains around Banff and Lake Louise.

At the end of that trip, when it was time to figure out my next, I realized that what I wanted to do was pitch myself to Open U.

Open U offered about three hundred different classes in everything from how to tap dance to how to build your own house. Thankfully, Sandy Bremer, the founder, was growing her organization and added me to her team. It was job Nirvana. We took bus trips to the Preakness, hosted disco dances, and organized adult education classes that teachers hosted in their homes. (Those were more trusting times.) We even ran running groups where we met on the mall by the Smithsonian and trained together for 10K road races (followed by a celebratory brunch).

I had agreed to a salary that was less than half of what I'd been making before because I believed in their mission, loved the work, and thought I would soon get a raise as a result of my hustle and active role in boosting revenue.

Well, three months went by. Six months went by. I was working long hours, coming up with new course ideas, and writing copy that was increasing registrations. I kept waiting for a call to the office to get a word of praise, a pat on the back, a promotion, a raise. Something. Nothing.

After a year of this, I felt like I was being taken advantage of. I wasn't getting paid what I thought I was worth. I was even considering leaving because I thought this was so unfair. I finally decided to speak up for myself. I stormed into Sandy's office (forgive me, I was young), pounded my fist on her desk, and said, "I think I deserve a raise."

She looked at me calmly and said, "You're right, you do. I was wondering when you were going to have the courage to come in and ask for it."

Sandy was right. It was *not* her responsibility to give me a raise. It was *my* responsibility to ask for one if I thought I earned it and if I had evidence of the bottom-line value I had added.

I'm grateful to Sandy Bremer, for many things. She was a wonderful boss who taught me a lot, including that it is up to us to ask for what we deserve. If we don't ask, the answer's always no.

How about you? Are you in a situation where you're not getting what you deserve? Are you waiting for someone to initiate on your behalf? You might be waiting a long time.

If you've gotten any message from this book, I hope it's this: Our happiness is in our hands. If we don't like what's happening, it's up to us to do something about it. Speaking of which, when we're unhappy with something, there really are only four things we can do about it.

Unhappy? You Can Avoid, Argue, Accept, or Alter

"Control your own destiny or someone else will."
—JACK WELCH

I was talking about this with my friend Glenna during our monthly phone call and she said, "Sam, you know there are only four things we can do when we're unhappy with a situation, right?" We can:

Avoid: We can suppress it, deny it, or pretend whatever is bothering us is a non-issue.

Argue: We can get upset and complain about what's happening to others or the perpetrator.

Accept: We can decide it's "just the way it is" and there's nothing we can do about it.

Alter: We can take action to improve it, stop it, or prevent it from happening again.

A favorite example of someone who decided to *alter* her situation instead of *avoid* it, *accept* it, or *get angry* about it is a female engineer who worked in the space industry. As a new mom, she was feeling guilty because she wasn't "there" for her baby. She was tired of breast pumping in a cramped bathroom at work and was torn by conflicting loyalties to her job and son. She realized she was fortunate to have a prestigious position where she was challenged, but she was considering quitting even though the loss of income would put a serious dent in the family budget.

After weeks of feeling frazzled, she realized she had been dealing with all this in her head and hadn't given management a chance to improve the situation. She prepared a proposal requesting reduced hours and asking that a "new mom room" be set up at work so she (and other new moms) could breast-pump or have break time in clean, private surroundings.

Her boss didn't even have to think about it. She did such a thorough job showing why they could trust that her work responsibilities would get done in thirty hours, and why it was a smart financial move to honor their female employees with a private room, he said "yes" on the spot.

This turned into a win for her and her employer. It prevented an unnecessary, unwelcome "talent/knowledge drain" and the loss of a valued employee—and she got the best of all worlds.

How about you? Are you on the verge of quitting something because circumstances aren't what you want, need, or deserve? Could you put together a proposal that recommends a win-win solution for you and your employer? Could you approach your decision maker and ask for what you *do* want instead of "voting with your feet" because you're getting what you *don't* want?

Use These Five Principles of Successful Persuasion to Get a Yes to Your Request

"Believe in yourself. Even if you don't, pretend you do,
and at some point, you will."

—VENUS WILLIAMS

You may be thinking, "I know it's time for me to speak up for what I want. I'm just not sure how to do it in a way that gets a yes." The good news is, there are steps you can take to make a solid business case for your request. These Five Principles of Persuasion can help turn resistance into receptivity—whether you are negotiating a raise or asking your team leader to improve a situation that is undermining the morale and productivity of you and others in the office.

Persuasion Principle #1: Believe in the value of what you're proposing.

You may think this is obvious. Well, as my dad used to say, "Just because something is common sense doesn't mean it's common practice." Have you ever made a request while harboring secret doubts, "This is a waste of time; they'll never approve this?" If you don't believe your proposal stands a chance, why should they?

Decision makers "bet on the jockey." They need to trust you know what you're doing before they approve your proposal. Repeatedly tell yourself, "I know this is worthwhile, a win for all involved," *before* walking into the room so you exude confidence.

Persuasion Principle #2: Anticipate why they might say no and say it first.

Determine why they might reject your request and bring it up first. If you don't, they won't even be listening to you; they'll be waiting for their turn to talk so they can tell you why this won't work. If you predict they'll protest with, "We tried this before and it didn't work," guess what the first words out of your mouth better be? "You may be thinking we tried this before and it backfired. You're right, and that's why we identified where this went wrong last time and put systems in place to prevent it from happening again."

Persuasion Principle #3: Number your points.

My high-school debate coach used to tell us, "Your expertise is perceived by the organization of your thoughts. What you're proposing may be valid, but if your points are confusing, decision makers will conclude you don't know what you're talking about." The easiest and quickest way to lend legitimacy to your points is to number them. "There are three reasons this will be a money-saver for the company. The first is . . . The second is . . . The third is . . ." People are more likely to understand and respect what we're saying when we put it in an easy-to-follow-and-remember structure.

Persuasion Principle #4: Use *their* language and focus on *their* needs.

Avoid using the word "I," as in "I think" or "I want" or "I need." People, especially decision makers in business, do things for *their* reasons, not *yours*. A columnist named Paul Harlan Collins illustrated how parents have become a master at this. "If you want your teenager to shovel the driveway, tell him he can use the car. If you want to teach your kids to count, give them different allowances."

Ask yourself, "What's most important to the person I'm trying to persuade?" Money? Safety? Reputation? Relationships? Health? Employee loyalty? Productivity? Figure out how your proposal will benefit them and address those advantages. If what's important to your boss is maintaining market share or a competitive edge, emphasize how implementing this innovation will help the company stand out in a crowded marketplace and attract new customers.

Persuasion Principle #5: Create a two-way conversation.

No one likes to be lectured. If we pressure people to see the wisdom of our arguments, they may say no simply because they don't like being ordered around. People like to make up their own minds. The goal is to actively engage them with "Wouldn't it be wonderful if . . . ?" questions so they're picturing what we're proposing. Now they're seeing what we're saying. They're halfway to agreeing to it because they're imagining it as if it's a done deal.

One of the reasons that female engineer's boss said yes to the changes she proposed was because she used these Five Rules of Persuasion. How about you? If you're ready to speak up for what you want, need and deserve, make a bottom-line business case for why saying yes to your request is in the best interests of all involved.

Lucille Ball said, "I'd rather regret the things I've done than regret the things I haven't done." Keep that in mind next time you're not getting what you want. You'll never regret speaking up and negotiating for what you want; you'll only regret passively accepting less than you deserve.

INNOVATE a Fresh Start

"You may have a fresh start any moment you choose,
for this thing we call 'failure' is not the falling down,
but the staying down."

—MARY PICKFORD

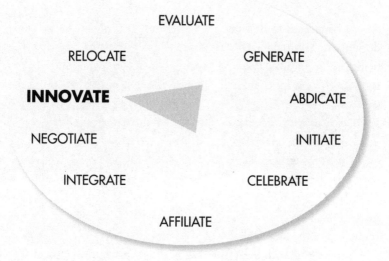

EVALUATE

RELOCATE   GENERATE

INNOVATE   ABDICATE

NEGOTIATE   INITIATE

INTEGRATE   CELEBRATE

AFFILIATE

Have you taken action on the previous Life Hacks, yet there is still a situation in your life that is not to your liking? Life Hack 9 shows additional ways to *alter* a soul-sucking situation instead of *accept* it, *avoid* it, *argue* about it, or get *angry* about it. You'll discover it's never too late to INNOVATE a fresh start, regardless of what you're dealing with.

24

Quit Watering Dead Plants

"I'm just trying to think about the future and not be sad."
— ELON MUSK

att walked in the door and plopped down on the stairs. I had never seen anyone look so dejected. I said, "Matt, no twenty-five-year-old should ever look like that. What's up?"

Matt was living in my basement, working part-time for me while working full-time for an association. He was saddled with college debt and living very frugally to pay it down.

"I went for my performance review today. I shared some ideas with my boss on how we could clean up a couple of our systems so they're more efficient. I even developed some spreadsheets to show how it would work and how much money they would save."

"So, what happened?"

"She said, 'Matt, that's not what you're getting paid to do. Just do your job.'"

He looked so heartbroken, I asked, "Matt, what do you want to do? What's your dream?"

"I can't even think about dreaming until I pay off these loans and that's years from now."

I said, "Dreaming costs nothing. Not dreaming costs everything. What would you do if you could?"

"Well, I follow a lot of travel bloggers. I'd love to do what they do."

"Why don't you pick out a few favorites and reach out to them? Say, 'I know you're busy, and if you had one piece of advice for someone who wants to do what you do, what would it be?'"

Suffice it say, Matt did reach out to his favorite adventure travelers. One said a good video camera was an essential tool of the trade and recommended which one to get. The other suggested he start local by blogging and videoing excursions to interesting places and events in the area. And in his spare time, that's exactly what Matt did.

Guess where Matt is now? South Korea. He initially taught ESL and is now a manager for a search firm. He has scuba-dived, zip-lined, and explored countries he never would have visited otherwise. All because he stopped watering dead plants. Instead of staying stuck in a soul-sapping job, or withdrawing and retreating in despair, he set his dream in motion.

Notice, for the first few years, *Matt was still paying off his college loans,* but while experiencing overseas adventures and doing rewarding work where he was appreciated.

Are You Sad About Your Future? It's Not Too Late for a Fresh Start

"A time comes when you need to stop waiting for the man you want to become and start being the man you want to be."

— BRUCE SPRINGSTEEN

How about you? Do you feel, as Matt did initially, sad about your future? Have you lost hope?

You have a choice. You can withdraw and retreat—or you can reach out. As George Eliot said, "It is never too late to be who what might have been." You can dream even when in discouraging circumstances. In fact, dreams can be your saving grace. They are a way to mentally escape an unsatisfying situation in and envision a way out.

Like Miki Agrawal did by first noticing how unhealthy restaurant food was, which motivated her to wonder if there might be healthier options, which motivated her to GTS the topic, which led to her decision to start a farm-to-table restaurant.

That all started with an idea in *her* head. A better future starts with an idea in *your* head.

But first, you've got to believe it is not "foolish" to dream in tough times. It's often the first step to getting out of them. As the lyrics in the Oscar Hammerstein II song *Happy Talk* go, "If you don't have a dream, how you gonna make a dream come true?"

Audrey Niffenegger, author of *The Time Traveler's Wife* said, "We all have time machines. Some take us back. Those are called memories. Some take us forward. Those are called dreams."

Remember the W5 Form we discussed in "Put a Date on the Calendar" (chapter 5, page 48)? Did you fill it out? Post it? If not, it's not too late. If you want your dream to be a time machine that improves your quality of life, fill out that W5 Form today and put it where you'll see it every day.

Do You Feel Like You're Hitting Your Head Against a Wall?

"The most common way people give up their power is by thinking they don't have any."

— ALICE WALKER

A salon attendee asked, "How do we know when we're watering a dead plant?"

I told her, "You know you are watering a dead plant when it feels you've been hitting your head against a wall for months (or years) and the situation hasn't improved. If you've done everything you can to improve a situation, if you've examined yourself to see how you might be contributing to this situation, changed your approach, done your best to offer proactive solutions, and this situation *still* hasn't gotten better, it's time to stop watering that plant."

Fresh starts don't happen by themselves. It's up to you to initiate them.

A millennial named Lisa told me, "I have been lobbying for a leadership role in my association for two years, but my manager is very controlling. I think he sees me as a threat and keeps blocking my promotions. I like my work other than this frustration of not being able to move up the ranks. I didn't want to quit; I just wanted to run something.

"My mom suggested I get involved in our local Chamber of Commerce so I checked it out. At first I thought it wouldn't be a match because the members are a lot older than me, but my mom said this was a chance to make it more relevant to the younger business owners in our area.

"They made me feel welcome from the first meeting. In fact, they made me Program Chair three months after I joined. Now I'm President Elect. I get to plan events and bring in really interesting speakers. For example, last month we had a panel of food truck owners. One guy was a military veteran who never dreamed he'd be able to own his own business in his hometown. It's so rewarding to have people appreciate my leadership, instead of trying to squash it."

Know When to Fold 'Em

> "If at first you don't succeed, try, try, again. Then quit.
> There's no use being a damn fool about it."
>
> —W. C. FIELDS

How about you? Are you in a deadend situation where you're not appreciated and you can read the writing on the wall—and it's not going to get better no matter what you do? Are you in a toxic relationship and the other person isn't open, interested, or willing to change?

It might be time to get rid of the plant. From an early age, it's drummed into us that we should never, ever give up. We're taught winners never quit. That persevering is the stuff of champions. Tenacity is indeed a valuable quality, to a point. As with anything, it can be taken to an extreme.

Cyndi and Ed Justice are a case in point. While in Hawaii, I had the privilege of visiting Talk Story Bookstore. This world-famous store is located on Hawaii's least-visited major island and in an out-of-the-way town of less than three thousand people. Yet it has been one of the state's fastest-growing businesses for the past five years. Trip Advisor says it's the #1 visitor destination on Kauai.

How can this be? In one word . . . clarity. Clarity about what they stand for and what they won't stand for. Ed and Cyndi visited Kauai on their honeymoon and liked it so much, they decided to take a leap of faith and put their money where their dream was. They didn't have a background in the book biz and didn't plan on buying a bookstore. Yet they made money from the first day they opened their doors because their motto is "Don't follow rules, follow values."

For example, the "rules" say a brick and mortar store has to have a cash register, right? The problem is, cash registers lock you into one location, usually in a front corner of your store. But what if there are customers in back who can't find what they want? If no one's around to answer their question or make recommendations, they often leave and don't return.

That's why Ed and Cyndi "quit" their cash register six months after they opened. They now wear cash belts around their waist, which gives them freedom to connect with customers. While I was there, they greeted every single person who walked in the store. One of them was always out on the floor, asking people what they were looking for and pointing out similar authors in their preferred genre.

The trend in the bookselling industry these days is to diversify in order to grow. They added a café, an art gallery, book clubs, open mic nights, and comfortable chairs so people could sit and read.

Guess what they discovered? Those extra services created lots of problems and didn't sell books. In fact, Cyndi said, "We were coming in at six a.m. and staying until ten p.m. We found *Coffee sells coffee. Books sell books.* So, we quit diversifying and went back to what worked for us."

As we talked, it was clear that the secret sauce to their success was they *quit watering dead plants.* They said, "No, thank you," to anything that *didn't* make money and *didn't* bring them joy. Doing that freed up time and money for what *did* bring them money and joy.

I told them, "There's a (perhaps apocryphal) story about Michelangelo who, when asked how he created his masterpiece sculpture, supposedly said, *'I just chipped away everything that wasn't David.'* Kudos to you for 'David-ing' your life. You've chipped away everything that isn't congruent with your Top Priorities. As a result, you're successful for all the right reasons."

How about you? If you're unhappy, could it be because you're following everyone else's rules and not your own? Are you watering dead plants? What do you need to quit in order to get back in alignment with what's right for you?

If You Can't Quit, How Can You Compensate?

"You may have been given a cactus, but you don't have to sit on it."
—JOYCE MEYER

When I lived on Oahu, I offered a course on "Confidence" for the University of Hawaii. I will always remember Lana, one of the participants, because of her story. She had been accepted to University of Southern California Film School, her dream, and loved every minute of it. Then, both her parents got sick and, as their only child, she returned to the islands to take care of them. The only job she could find was at the post office. She was miserable. She didn't fit in and was not particularly good at her job. She was a creative person stuck with a mind-numbing sorting job. She didn't see any light at the end of this tunnel. Lana said, "I don't even know who I am anymore."

I asked, "What did you used to love to do?"

"I was born to be a filmmaker. I was in my element at USC learning how to make documentaries. My professors told me I really had talent. It kills me to feel I've abandoned that."

"Is there any way you can contact the local PBS station and see if they need volunteers? I know you don't have much free time; however, maybe they need help with one of their projects?"

That's what she did. I can still see her face, wreathed in a smile, when she walked in for our final session. I asked what happened and she said that someone at the PBS station had put her in touch with the Hawaii International Film Festival. At that point, she didn't even know what she was going to do for them, but she knew she was going to do something. It was just what she needed to give her a light at the end of the very dark tunnel she was in.

I call this the Godfather Plan. If you really are locked in and have no options, make your mind a deal it can't refuse. You can accept less-than-ideal circumstances if you understand *why* you're doing this and if you give yourself *something* that makes you happy in exchange.

Are you in a dark tunnel? Even if you only have an hour a week, how can you bring back something you enjoy to give yourself a much-needed fresh start?

You've probably heard the phrase "It was a light at the end of the tunnel." In the midst of dark times, we don't just need a light at the *end* of the tunnel; we need a light *in* the tunnel right now. Doing something that puts the light on in our eyes is one way to do that.

What Could Be a Light in Your Tunnel Right Now?

"Keep your face to the sunshine and you cannot see the shadow."
— HELEN KELLER

I have a friend who's in a tunnel right now. Her husband has been dealing with nonstop back pain for years. He's no longer able to work and is on constant pain meds that compromise his ability to work, drive, and get around. She was left a property by a family member, but the property was in a demoralizing state of decay and saddled with tax liens and attorney bills. Instead of this being a much-needed financial windfall to go toward their ever-mounting medical bills, it will take months of legal wrangling that will drain the property of any value.

How does she stay strong in the face of all this? How does she keep going? I was at her office the other day and commented on the incredibly beautiful music she was listening to. "Oh," she said, "Tuesday is acapella day. We play Straight No Chaser and barbershop music. Monday is Country. Big Band music is on Thursdays and we play Oldies But Goodies on Friday."

I thought, "Little things can make a big difference." I admire her for doing the best she can under the circumstances. One thing that keeps her going is music, so she makes it part of her daily life.

What keeps you going in dark times?

For some people, it's sunlight. I remember, not fondly, the long winters in Washington, D.C., and how bleak they made me feel. Then I read an article that the National Institutes of Health had just identified something they called SAD—seasonal affective disorder. They listed the symptoms (sluggishness, loss of interest in activities you normally enjoy, social withdrawal, craving for foods high in carbohydrates) and I thought, "Aha. So this funk isn't just all in my head."

All I knew is that in the gray, rainy, sleety days from December to March, I felt like a bear who wanted to hibernate. This study showed that some people really do feel gloomy on gray days because loss of sunlight causes a drop in serotonin and melatonin that disrupts mood and sleep.

You can counteract some of the effects of SAD with light therapy. Check with your doctor first to see if a "light box" is appropriate for you. Barring that, good old sunshine (especially at the beginning of your day) can boost your metabolism and immunity, provide Vitamin D and D_3, and contribute to healthy bones and eyes. It can, literally, make you happier and healthier.

This may sound simplistic, however the goal is to remember while we may not be able to change the big things in our life, we *can* change the little things and they add up.

If You Can't Change Your Circumstances, Change Your Mindset

"In a world where you can be anything, be kind."

—Connie Schultz

I had an opportunity to speak on National Library Day for a group of library professionals. Their district coordinator was so smart in how he opened the program. He had reached out to patrons in the weeks before the event and asked, "How have our librarians made a difference for you?"

He took a stack of letters from grateful patrons to the stage, sat in a chair, and started reading. There were tears in the room as he read story after story of people who said their lives had been changed because a librarian had gone above and beyond on their behalf.

"I got a job because you helped me with my résumé." "Thank you for being so kind to me and calling me by my name every time I walk in. It's the only place I feel welcome." "I am the first from our family to go to college. I'm now a proud Johns Hopkins grad and a reference librarian because *your* reference librarian showed me we can learn anything if we're willing to look it up."

When it was my turn to speak, even though I hadn't originally planned to tell this story, I spontaneously decided to add it to the mix. "I grew up in a small town with more horses than people. In fact, I rode my horse, a rangy Palomino called Joe, to the library and tied him up outside while I went in to see if there were any new books I hadn't already read. I will always be grateful to Mrs. Price for introducing me to Walter Farley's *Black Stallion* series. The books she recommended introduced me to a big world out there waiting to be explored beyond our isolated mountain valley. I only wish I could thank her for the pivotal role she played in my life. One reason I'm an author is because she cared enough to invest time in a ten-year-old kid."

A librarian told me after my talk, "I've been doing this for twenty-three years. I was on the verge of quitting because the job has changed so much since I started. Many days I'm more of a cop than a librarian. It seems all I do is get asked, 'Where's the bathroom?' and field complaints about people hogging the computer. Hearing those letters and your story reminded me why I got into this profession in the first place."

How about you? If you're in a situation with elements you can't control (loved ones in pain, people hogging the computer), what *can* you control? The amount of sunshine you get? Playing music that lifts your spirits? Focusing on the difference you're making? If you're in the midst of dark times, doing something that shines a light on what's right isn't petty; it's pivotal.

Michelle Obama said, "We need to do a better job of putting ourselves higher on our to-do list." In the next chapter, we discuss why doing the opposite of your always is a wonderful way to start putting yourself higher on your to-do list.

25

Do the Opposite of Your Always

Lucy: "Do you think anyone ever really changes?"
Linus: "I've changed a lot in the last year."
Lucy: "I mean for the better."

—CHARLES M. SCHULTZ

was in Costa Rica speaking to a group of transformational leaders. Many were highly successful—but at a price. They were always on the road, in an airport, or hosting some kind of program at a far-away hotel. I told them, "One of the reasons I decided to launch my Year by the Water adventure was because I realized my life had become an aircraft carrier."

"A what?!" someone in the front row asked.

I told the group, "In my twenties, I dated a Navy pilot who flew off carriers. I remember him telling me, 'You know how you stop an aircraft carrier? You don't. It has so much mass and momentum, it keeps going even after you turn off the engines. You can put the engines in full reverse and it still takes up to four miles for the carrier to come to a stop.'"

To me, that was a metaphor waiting to happen. I'd been doing the same kind of work for decades. My career had become an aircraft carrier, a good one, but it had accumulated so much self-perpetuating mass and momentum, I was going to keep heading in the direction I was heading.

The thing is, it's a big ocean out there. There are ports I've never seen. Parts of the ocean I haven't explored. Did I want to just keep steaming along—or change things up?

How about you? Have your career and life become an aircraft carrier? Do you want to continue doing what you've always done, going in the direction you are now? Or is it time to jump ship?

A well-known author put his hand up and said, "I can't afford to jump ship. I have a lot of people depending on me. I kind of owe it to them to keep this carrier going."

"I understand this is a conundrum. You might be interested to hear what George R. R. Martin says about this," and I started reading an excerpt from a *Daily Mash* interview with the *Game of Thrones* author:

> "I was a hundred thousand words into Winds of Winter. I've got armies in one continent, zombies in another, dragons burning things all over the place, and numerous uninteresting sub-plots involving minor noblemen whose names I cannot currently recall. It is, by anyone's reckoning, a . . . nightmare.
>
> "I was looking at several more months of inhumanly hard graft and even then everyone is bound to slag it off as 'unsatisfying.'
>
> "Meanwhile it is a lovely day outside and I am an older man with more money than I can possibly ever spend. You tell me why I should finish this? It's an honest question. Someone else can do it if they like, I'm cool with that."

Wow. GRRM (as he's referred to in the biz) was considering *jumping ship*. As you can imagine, his publisher, producer, and millions of fans were pressuring him not to. The question is, "Whose life is it anyway?"

After dedicating decades to creating a series that has delighted people around the world and made millions of dollars—for him and others—does he have the right to do what he wants at this stage of his career and life? Does he have the right to put his obligations to others aside and enjoy the lovely day outside? Who is he beholden to? His fans and followers? Or himself?

Is It Time to Change Direction?

"Unless you change your direction, you'll end up where you're headed."
—LAO TZU

And you? Will you keep doing what you're doing because people are relying on you to? At what cost? Do you have the right to do what *you* want? Is that selfish? Whose life is it, anyway?

Even if your life and career are headed in good directions, are they the same directions they've been going in for decades? Is it time to explore areas of the ocean you haven't yet seen?

There are options, of course.

You don't have to jump ship. Maybe you can just fly off the carrier now and then to take side trips. Maybe you can turn the carrier in new directions, explore different parts of the ocean, stop in new ports. What do you think?

That quote from GRRM created a fascinating discussion with those leaders because it articulated what some of them felt. They too were in the second half of their careers. Many had fame and fortune. They were leading *the* good life. Meanwhile it was a sunny day outside and some didn't have the freedom to enjoy it. They had places to go, ballrooms to fill.

One told me later, "I wish I could go off the grid for a little while and then come back. I'm tired of rushing from one city to the next. I just want to go out to dinner without being interrupted by someone asking for a selfie. I know it sounds simplistic, but I want to get up in the morning and water my garden. I'm only home two or three days a month and I never get to do that."

You may be thinking this smacks of privilege or first-world problems and that you'd happily switch places with these individuals and they can try living your life for a while.

I get it. Please understand. They know how fortunate they are. In fact, that's why they were initially reluctant to even say anything out loud because they didn't want to come across as whiners or ungrateful complainers.

The point is this. The only way to sustain a life of service . . . is to also serve yourself.

How about you? Are you ready to fly off the carrier for some well-deserved sidetrips, but you're afraid to say anything lest you come across as being ungrateful?

If so, revisit the Serve Others–Serve Ourselves Continuum (see page 96) to see if you're out of balance. And if you are, it's time to get creative about options you may not have considered.

There Are Other Ways to Fly Off the Carrier

"I want adventure in the great wide somewhere."

—BELLE, IN *BEAUTY AND THE BEAST*

A thirty-something couple, both entrepreneurs with their own business, told me, "Your Year by the Water inspired us to 'fly off the carrier' for three months last year. We became snowbirds!"

"How so?"

"We live in a refurbished church in Brooklyn, just across the river from New York City. Everything we want is right out our front door. Several friends live on the same floor so we have a built-in community. It's perfect nine months a year. The other three months, uhh, not so much. We can do without the snowstorms, black ice, and freezing cold. Someone suggested we rent our place in winter and go somewhere sunny, like Southern California. At first, we thought this was something retirees did, but we discovered a lot of entrepreneurs are doing it because they can run their businesses from just about anywhere."

"How did you make it work?"

"We had weekly Skype meetings with our team, which gave them the freedom to work from home too. We Airbnb'd our place in NYC, and the money from that covered rent in both places and our airfare there and back. We got to keep our home and community in Booklyn, make new friends, and experience a whole new lifestyle in Venice Beach. A triple bottom-line win."

Where Can You Go to Get Away?

"Every woman needs a room of her own."

—Virginia Woolf

You may be thinking, "Well, good for them. But I've got a family and there's no way we're going to Airbnb our home for three months a year and become snowbirds."

Want to know another way to get away—and it's nearby and free?

Find a Third Place. What's a Third Place? Well, the science of ergonomics (the study of how our environment influences our effectiveness) states your home is your First Place and where you work is your Second Place. If you run a business out of your home, that's your First *and* Second Place. Ergonomic experts say it's difficult to stay focused on creative projects in your First and Second Place because your environment keeps reminding you of the laundry, bills, client work, or household chores you customarily do in that space.

Your *Third Place*, e.g., a nearby coffee shop, bookstore or your local library, is a *public* place where you can work in *private*. Think about your neighborhood. Is there a deli or café that has some tables in the back where you can work in public-private?

Plan on going there for an hour or two sometime this week. Promise yourself you will not check email or social media in your Third Place. It is only for creative work. And buy a meal, tip the staff, and go at off hours so you're not freeloading or taking up tables customers will want.

Working in your Third Place not only gives you a "room of your own," so to speak, it kick-starts that sublimely productive state of flow for several reasons.

1) Does the name Pavlov ring a bell? If working on your creative project is the *only* thing you do in your Third Place, it sets up a *repeat ritual* where the faucet of flow opens up every time you walk in because creating is what's associated with that environment.

2) You're not constantly interrupted by people asking you to cook dinner, find their backpack, or answer "one quick question."

3) Instead of working in isolation and having to provide all your own energy, you can piggyback off the energy of others in the room. This socializes the creative process without any of the downsides because people aren't disturbing you.

4) You finally have a place where you can make your *creative* priority your *top* priority.

What's Your Third Place?

"Some people have analysis. I have Utah."

— Robert Redford

A writer told me her Third Place has become her saving grace. She said, "I attended your workshop at the San Francisco Writers Conference. You told us that Jacquelyn Mitchard wrote *The Deep End of the Ocean*, Oprah's first Book Club pick, at her kitchen table during the day while her kids were at school.

"That inspired me, so after I dropped my kids off at school, I sat down at the kitchen table and tried to write, but the dirty dishes kept screaming at me and I kept checking the refrigerator to grab a snack and see what I wanted to make for dinner.

"Then, I remembered what you said about the Third Place. I started stopping at a Panera Bread that's on the way back from their school that actually welcomes telecommuters. There's always a handful of people in there working on their laptops. I got more done on my book in the last two months than I have in the last two years. Plus, it *has* become a ritual. The staff knows what kind of coffee I like and they start fixing it as soon as they see me walk in the door."

I love her story because it shows there can be simple fixes to what frustrates us. She loved her family, yet she had put her writing dreams on hold because she felt she just didn't have the bandwidth to do both. Instead of waiting until her kids went off to college, going to her Third Place has given her a way to serve her family *and* her creative dream.

Ask Yourself, "What Could Provide Contrast?"

"We are so made that we can derive intense enjoyment only from a contrast."

— SIGMUND FREUD

If you're still not clear how to fly off your carrier, you might want to follow Harry's example.

While in Morro Bay, California, I like to stay at the Harbor House Inn because it's owned and operated by an Indian family who take great pride in running a hotel that's a "home away from home." I asked Harry (who lives with his wife in a one-room suite next to the registration desk), "I know running a hotel is a 24/7 operation. What would you do if you could take a day off?"

He paused for a moment and then said, "I wouldn't know what to do with myself."

I said, "One way to figure out what we *want* to do is to do the *opposite* of what we *always do.*"

"What do you mean?"

"I had an opportunity years ago to meet Arthur Frommer, the travel legend who wrote the *Europe on $5 a Day* series. I asked him, 'You've visited the Taj Mahal, the Great Wall. What's your favorite place to go?' and he said, 'My backyard.'"

I was intrigued, "Why, of all the places in the world, is that your favorite?"

"He told me, 'The purpose of a vacation is to *provide contrast.* If you're around people all the time, your ideal vacation may be to go to a deserted island. I travel all the time, so in my off-time, what makes me happy is to stay home and do nothing.'"

Harry told me, "Hmm, doing nothing would be nice. That is definitely a contrast to my norm."

I asked, "What else?"

Harry said, "I would go to Montaña del Oro and hike all day."

"Got it. You. Mother Nature. Being outside in the sunshine. Not being at people's beck and call. Not checking people in. Not fixing leaky faucets or TV remotes that won't work."

Harry's answer was in alignment with what Carl Jung said, "The greater the contrast, the greater the potential. Great energy only comes from a correspondingly great tension of opposites."

So, what is the opposite of your always? That might be exactly what you need to take a satisfying break and, as Harry told me, "come back fresh."

What could you do to give yourself some contrast? Could a local Third Place become your Utah? Could you work on a creative project at your local library so you have a ritual and a room of your own . . . now, not later?

And if none of those are options, read on. It may be time to get a new carrier.

LIFE HACK 10

RELOCATE to Greener Pastures

"The real voyage of discovery consists not in seeking new landscapes, but in having new eyes."

— MARCEL PROUST

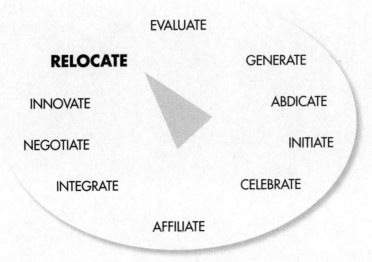

So, our final Life Hack. If you've tried everything else, and your life is still not what you want it to be, it may be time to RELOCATE and move out and move on. Sometimes the grass is green enough right where we are, sometimes it really is greener elsewhere. Contrary to what Proust said, sometimes the best way to develop new eyes *is* to seek new landscapes.

26

Give Yourself a GFS— Geographic Fresh Start

"I wish I'd had the courage to live a life true to myself, not the life others expected of me."
—#1 REGRET OF THE DYING, AS REPORTED
BY PALLIATIVE NURSE BONNIE WARE IN *THE GUARDIAN*

A woman with a friendly face saw me peering in the window of the small café in San Miguel de Allende in Mexico. I was there to speak at a writers' conference and was out walking the cobblestone streets looking for some breakfast and a cup of coffee.

She got up out of her chair, came over, opened the door, and waved me in. "Come on in. I live in the neighborhood and eat here every day. You hit the jackpot."

Which is how I met Gael Sherman and got to hear her inspiring story. "I retired and divorced, amicably, about the same time. Back then you could get a round-the-world-in-a-year ticket for $4,000, which I could just afford on my teacher's pension. I was inspired by Rita Golden

Gelman's book *Tales of a Female Nomad* to grab my backpack and hit the road.

"Thanks to her, I discovered organizations like Servas International (an extension of the UN's peace-giving mission) and WWOOF (World-wide Opportunities on Organic Farms), which provided hosts in countries around the world. I even wrote a blog about my travels, 'Notes from Gael's Mid-life Walkabout.' This was back in 2004 so it was hard to find WiFi then. I spent many hours in Internet cafés posting segments of my blog because there was intermittent service and not enough bandwidth to send it out all at once."

I asked, "How did you end up in San Miguel?"

"When I got back to Austin, it had changed and, in my opinion, not for the better. I started coming to San Miguel for two weeks at a time, then two months, then finally decided to go all-in and make it permanent. There are more than a hundred nonprofits in the area. I started working with kids who have disabilities and now co-operate a school for the blind."

I asked what many people asked me about "being away from home." "Do you ever get lonely?"

"Nope. There's plenty to do. A lot of us are drawn here because it's an artist's colony and we finally get to paint, sculpt, or write, something we never got to do in our former life."

"What would you want people to know about traveling or relocating?"

She laughed, "Other than 'Just *do* it?!'" She thought about it for a moment then said with real urgency, "The world is *friendly*. I would tell people to stop seeing people in different countries as 'the other.' As the saying goes, strangers are just friends you haven't met yet."

Exactly. A gentleman at a nearby table came over after Gael left and said, "My name is Richard. I couldn't help but overhear your conversation. Mind if I join you?"

I agreed and asked him about his life as an ex-pat. He said, "People from the states often tell me, 'I could never leave my family behind. Don't you miss them?' I tell them, 'Look, I'm eighty-two years old. My kids have their own lives. I'm what you call a secondary feature. Even if I moved back to the states, I'd see them every few months. I can see them every few months *here*. Plus, we stay connected with FaceTime, so I really don't think of it as leaving them behind.'"

Richard had just articulated a key distinction. Moving someplace new doesn't have to mean you leave loved ones *behind*. It often means, as I discovered during my Year by the Water, that you have the best of both worlds. You get to stay connected with loved ones via text, photos, phone calls, emails, and Skype videos and, *at the same time*, explore new places where the stars kiss the ocean. To me, this is wealth in what really matters.

Is There a Better Place for You?

"Every exit is an entry somewhere else."

—TOM STOPPARD

Gael, Richard, and the many ex-pats I met who have relocated to new homes and countries are walking-talking role models attesting to the fact that sometimes the grass *is* greener elsewhere.

Gael and Richard were no longer happy where they were. So, they moved out and moved on.

Are you happy where you are? Are you a roots person who prefers to stay in one place, who values the stability and familiarity? If so, good for you.

If not, what are you doing about it?

As discussed throughout this book, there *are* things you can do to improve your quality of life, right where you are. But if you're in a toxic place, or if you're unhappy or have "itchy feet," if you've tried everything to improve your situation and it hasn't helped, it might be time to find a new home that supports your happiness instead of sabotages it.

Environment matters. When we "stay put" it can be hard to change because everything and everyone in our current environment reminds us of who we've always been and how we've always been.

A woman named Jennifer told me, "My boyfriend and I broke up six months ago. I still can't stop thinking about him. Every time I'm in the living room, I think of all the time we spent curled up on our comfy couch, watching our favorite shows together. We're both foodies and every time I'm in the kitchen, I think of all the meals we prepared and fed each other. I get sad just walking in the front door, because the place feels so empty without him."

I asked, "Why don't you move to another apartment?"

She had a laundry list of reasons. She had a two-year lease. She didn't have a car. It would be a hassle to pack everything up and relocate.

"But if you're unhappy every single day, isn't it at least worth exploring whether there's a new place that could give you a geographical fresh start?"

She agreed it was worth checking out. Next time I heard from her, she was brimming with good news. "I found a one-bedroom on the river for the same rent. My landlord let me out of the lease because he had a waiting list of people wanting to live there. My new building has a gym downstairs and I've started working out every morning. Plus, my bedroom has a huge window facing east so I wake up to sunshine."

I asked, "What about your old boyfriend?"

Her eyebrows went up in surprise. "I don't even think about him anymore. I've moved on."

Look at what she said. She's *moved on*.

If You Want to Move On, Maybe It's Time to Move Out

> "You don't have to be sick to get better."
>
> — HALE IRWIN

Please understand, there doesn't need to be anything "wrong" for you to decide to move on. There wasn't anything "wrong" with my life when I headed off on my Year by the Water. I was just clear that as long as I stayed *where* I was, I would stay *who* I was.

As my son Andrew said, "I had created a life where I could do *any-thing* I wanted, and I wasn't taking advantage of it." I wanted to get up out of that chair, out from behind my desk, and become more active. I wanted to get out of same-old, same-old routines and shake things up. What better way to do that then to put myself in new situations that required new behaviors?

My friend Dianne, the psychologist, pushed back, saying, "But Sam, you're an extrovert who thrives on newness. Not everyone's like that. There are *roots* people and *wings* people. *Roots* people like familiarity and stability. *Wings* people prefer flexibility and variety."

"That's interesting. What do you mean?"

"*Roots* people often live in the same town all their life. They're often heavily involved in their community and spend the majority of their time with family members, neighbors, coworkers, or friends they grew up with. They derive a sense of security from staying *in* their comfort zone.

"*Wings* people enjoy getting *outside* their comfort zone. They often prefer to move around, to go to new places, meet new people. They thrive, and are most alive, when they're mixing things up."

I laughed and said, "That reminds me of my friend Ruth's story. She grew up in England and was hired right out of college as a professor at her alma mater. She was a bright and shining star for them, but it was still a surprise when her dean burst into her office a few years later and said, "I've got wonderful news. You're the youngest professor to ever receive tenure in the history of this university! This is unprecedented. Just think, you've got a job for life."

Ruth told me, "Tenure?! The same job for the rest of my life. I was in my thirties. That was the last thing I wanted. It made me want to run for the hills." An interesting addendum to this story is that when Ruth went back for her twentieth college reunion, they had a global map with pins indicating the homes of alumni by the reception desk.

She said, "You've heard of the 80-20 Rule? Well, eighty percent of the pins were clustered within about thirty miles of the university. The vast majority of people were still close to where they grew up and went to school. The rest of the pins were spread around in countries spanning the globe."

Aha. A perfect example of roots and wings people.

Are You a Roots Person or a Wings Person?

"A good parent gives their child roots and wings."

—Jonas Salk

Are you a roots person who is happy where you are? If so, then by all means stay.

If you're unhappy, and have been unhappy for a long time, moving to a place more in alignment with your priorities may be just the geographical support you need to spread your wings.

One of my favorite examples of someone who did that is poet W. S. Merwin. As Executive Director of the Maui Writers Conference, I had an opportunity to interview Merwin at our very first Presenters' Reception. On a full-moon night, under the palm trees on Kapalua Beach, I asked, "What is one of the most important lessons learned from your career?"

I am paraphrasing here because I did not write down what he said (that'll teach me . . .), however, the gist of his remarks was that choosing to *concentrate on his craft* was the best decision he ever made on behalf of his career.

As the winner of a National Book Award and a Pulitzer Prize, Merwin received dozens of invitations to speaking engagements, book signings, and charity balls every week. Merwin realized it would be oh-so-easy to become part of the "glitterati" and that his work would suffer if he said yes to every request. He and his wife, Paula, were clear that continuing to live in NYC meant they would continue to be surrounded by temptations that would pull him away from the work he was born to do. So they moved to Maui to live a simpler, less distracting life, where he was freer to concentrate on his True Priorities.

I thought, "There's a man who knows what is important to him. He took responsibility for removing himself from an environment that was compromising what he valued most, and deliberately relocated to a place that supported him focusing on what will matter in the long run."

How about you? Is your current location toxic, but you're staying because you're afraid of the unknown? I hope this book has given you the tools to embrace uncertainty, be brave on your own behalf, and trust you can figure things out. I hope you've learned how to launch your priority project "in public" so people will jump on your bandwagon and contribute to its success.

If you've done everything to improve a current situation and the writing on the wall tells you it's not going to get better, heed the advice of palliative care nurse Bonnie Ware. Summon the courage to remove yourself from a place that's undermining your health and happiness. Seek a new home that supports your true self so you don't look back with regrets.

And yes, I know a major move can have major consequences, so I'm not suggesting you make a rash decision. An excellent resource for thinking this through from all angles is the book *Life Reimagined* by Richard J. Leider and Allan M. Webber. This book offers a variety of probing exercises to help you look at major life changes from all angles. I highly recommend it.

In the next chapter, you'll discover that relocating is not always to someplace new; sometimes it's coming full circle to where we were our best.

27

Come Full Circle

"One's destination is never a place,
but rather a new way of looking at things."

— HENRY MILLER

As I drove along the familiar windy road into this mountain valley, I still couldn't quite believe it had been thirty years since I'd been back to the small town where I grew up in Southern California.

Imagine the center of a triangle between Santa Maria, Ojai, and Taft, and that's where New Cuyama is nestled. As we used to say, more horses and oil rigs than people.

Marcel Proust felt it was smells that triggered remembrances of things past. For me, it's sights. There is the elementary school (two hundred students total) where Mr. Bowers, our elementary school librarian, gifted me with an identity by giving me a pen and ink drawing of a mustang, telling me that's what I was.

There is our tiny (twelve hundred square feet) three-bedroom home on Cebrian Street where we played with Barbie Dolls in tumbleweed forts in the backyard. There's the Buckhorn pool where Cheri defied our parents and changed into a (scandalous at the time) two-piece bathing suit at her thirteenth birthday party. There's the football field, home of many Friday Night Lights, where the whole town showed up to cheer on our six-man team. There's the ranch where our three hundred–pound pig (Ma Sow) jumped a three-foot fence and ran under the belly of my palomino horse Joe. That horse took off running and didn't come back for hours. There are the corrals where we kept our 4-H sheep and Future Farmers of America steers. When we begged our folks, "Do we have to feed them tonight? Can't we feed them in the morning?," they would give their standard response, "Do the right thing."

Thomas Wolfe got it wrong. Not only *can* we go home again, if we want to gain valuable insight into who and what shaped us and why, it's a trip worth taking. As Jennifer Lopez says, "No matter where I go, I know where I came from." Wise woman. Knowing "where we came from" can center us in who we really are, no matter how far away from home we are.

How Long Has It Been Since You've Gone Home?

"Home is where our story begins."
— ANNIE DANIELSON

Where did you grow up? Have you gone back there? What insights did your visit to the past reveal? Who came floating back to your memory as someone who has had enduring influence on you? What sights brought back family gatherings, good or not-so-good school experiences? What stories came to mind as you revisited the home of your upbringing?

Perhaps you're a roots person and you're still living where you grew up, or you return there frequently to visit family members and friends. This chapter may not be as relevant to you as it is to those who moved away from their hometown and haven't been back.

Country singer Kenny Chesney's decision to revisit his hometown catalyzed an unexpectedly rewarding new direction in his career. He made a surprise announcement to fans, concert organizers, and record producers that he was taking the summer off. Instead of doing his normal extremely lucrative concert tour, he was heading home to "recharge" his batteries and reconnect with his roots. His trip accomplished more than that. He visited his high-school football coach and was so inspired by their conversation that he developed a documentary about the impact of football and entitled it *The Boys of Fall*. He wrote the title song for the film and interviewed NFL stars Brett Favre, Tony Dungy, Peyton Manning, and Sean Payton. Chesney said, "Making this film was an incredible journey for me. It made me look at my life in a different way."

How about you? Could journeying "home" help you look at your life in a different way?

It did for musician Sting. Did you know Sting had writer's block for eight l-o-n-g years? As he said, "The words just wouldn't come. I was in a creative black hole." What did he do to remove that block? He returned to his English hometown near the shipyards of Newcastle, where he grew up watching "great iron ships grow until they blotted out the sun." He was so inspired by his conversations with the shipwrights, welders, riveters, and ship workers he ended up writing a Broadway musical called *The Last Ship* and performing in it. That creative rebirth might never have happened if he hadn't gone full circle and reconnected with his roots.

Could Going Back Help You Move Forward?

> "A man travels the world over in search of what
> he needs and returns home to find it."
> —George A. Moore

When and where were you your best self? Maybe your "home" isn't the place you grew up; maybe it was a time in your life you were in your element.

Such was the case of Neil Phillips, a charismatic individual who had been captain of the football team *and* basketball team at Harvard. He was recruited to be athletic director at his alma mater, Landon School, outside of Washington, D.C. Neil was revered there as a coach, public speaking instructor, and mentor and was promoted to headmaster (dean) of the entire school.

Dealing with the tumultuous lives of teens, many of whom had famous parents, was extremely nonstop demanding. He and his family lived on campus and the classes, sports, and school activities consumed him.

I met with Neil to discuss a potential book project. He was interested but had no spare time or energy. "Sam, Shannon, the kids, and I went to Florida for a week's vacation. We picnicked at a park one day that had a basketball court next to it. A guy drove up, got a ball from the trunk of his car, and started shooting hoops. And I just sat there. If you told me five years ago I wouldn't get up and play ball with a good player who was fifty yards away, I wouldn't have believed you."

I said, "Neil, what's your dream?"

"Don't get me wrong, I love my job, but what I've wanted to do for a long time is start an organization called Visible Men that gives young black boys positive adult role models."

I said, "Why aren't you doing that?"

"I don't want to let people down who are depending on me. Plus, I've got a family to support. Starting a nonprofit from scratch is a risk." He also wondered if he was going backward in his career to leave this highly respected position to launch a startup that had no guarantee of success.

I said, "Neil, I know you're serving people in your current job, but you *light up* every single time you talk about Visible Men. I think you were born to do this and you will end up serving even more people if you honor your instincts and do what you feel called to do."

Neil decided to host a basketball-camp fund-raiser that summer with fellow Harvard athlete, sportscaster James Brown. Putting a date on the calendar set the wheels in motion. Now, it was logistics, not good intentions. He found a location, recruited some coaches and players, and got the word out to kids in the area.

Guess what Neil is doing now? Well, go to the VisibleMen.org website and you will see the smiling faces of dozens of thriving students at Visible Men Academy in Sarasota, Florida. Watch the video of Neil speaking at the Nantucket Project. He is clearly doing his life's work.

How about you? Do you know what you want to do, but it seems like a step back? The best move forward is not always *more* money, *more* responsibility, *more* pressure, *more* prestige. Sometimes the best move forward is to go back to what really matters to you, back to what used to light you up, back to core values and where you think you can make the most difference.

What Will It Take for You to Live Up to Your Full Potential?

"What if, right at this very moment,
I am living up to my full potential?"

— LILY TOMLIN

I had the privilege of seeing Patty Stonesifer speak on a panel at the Do Good Fest ("Do Good. Be Good. Make Good") that featured individuals who were giving back to the community. Patty was the former Chief Executive Officer of Microsoft, overseeing more than 120,000 employees, and was then tapped to run the Bill and Melinda Gates Foundation, with $38 billion in assets.

What did Patty do when she was ready to move on to her next chapter? Did she scale up and head up another global organization? No, she accepted a job with a small nonprofit in Washington, D.C. The mission of Martha's Table is to "build a better future through healthy food, affordable clothing, and quality education."

Patty said, "People were shocked that I left such a high-powered position to serve as executive director for a local nonprofit. But here's what drove my decision. Do you know how many organizations there are in D.C. that serve the homeless? Forty-eight. And does the right hand know what the left hand is doing? No. Sometimes, three food trucks will pull up to the same location while people in another part of town go hungry. If we can't figure out how to solve poverty on a local level, how can we ever expect to solve it on a global level?"

There's a woman who decided the way to reach her full potential was to tackle a hands-on job to solve a problem at a grassroots level.

How about you? You know the saying, "Go big or go home"? Maybe it ought to be "Go home and go small."

Please understand, it's not regressing to go home if home is where you're in your wheelhouse. It's not a failure to choose something "smaller" if it's more in alignment with your purpose.

Is what's calling you a return to values that somehow got overshadowed along the way? Many of us have been taught to think progress means moving forward. Well, sometimes as Kenny Chesney and Sting found, it's better to move homeward. And as Patty Stonesifer found, sometimes, instead of living large, it's better to live local.

How about you? Have you been taught that growth is good? Grow your business. Grow your income. Grow your career. Grow your visibility. Sometimes that's true. And sometimes bigger isn't better. Sometimes, as we'll discuss in the next chapter, we're ready for . . . *contrast.*

You Don't Have to Go Home to Come Home

"A good traveler has no fixed plans and is not intent on arriving."
—LAO TZU

A number of people who heard about my travels said, "Oh, I could never be a nomad." A woman next to me at a famous breakfast place in Pawleys Island, South Carolina, said, "Doesn't being a vagabond get old? I would miss not having a home."

I told her, "The thing is, I *do* have a home. Home doesn't have to be a physical structure, and it doesn't have to be one place. Home is wherever I am."

She said, "I don't get that. To me, wandering from place to place sounds kind of aimless."

"To me, home is a state of mind. It reminds me of a story Ram Dass told. He was on a speaking tour with Timothy Leary, walked into yet another anonymous hotel room, looked around and no one was there. The room was empty. He felt empty and homesick. He decided to give himself a fresh start. He walked outside, then walked back in and called out, 'I'm home!'

"That's how I feel. I am not 'away' from home, *I am home* . . . in every sense of that word. Thanks to FaceTime, I am connected to the people I love wherever I go. And as long as I pay attention to my surroundings, I never feel empty or homesick. I feel connected, complete."

Come Home to Who You Are

"If you don't get out of the box you've been raised in,
you won't understand how much bigger the world is."

— ANGELINA JOLIE

How about you? Where is your physical home? Do you feel at home there? Or is it just a box you want to get out of?

Do you look forward to going home, coming home? If so, good for you.

If not, what can you do to feel more at home when you're home? Start doing your morning ritual? Clear away some of the clutter? Give who and what's there your full, fresh attention?

Could it be time to return to your hometown and rediscover your roots, core values, and True Priorities? Or is it time to find a new home?

Remember, home is not always a physical place. If you want to feel more comfortable in your own skin, come home to who you really are. If you do, you'll feel at home wherever you are.

I know that's a lot of "home" questions. It's just that home is where we feel we belong, where we feel connected. Being "at home" in our life is a prerequisite for liking our life. It matters.

As Oliver Wendell Holmes, Sr. pointed out, "Home is where we feel love, where our feet may leave, but not our hearts." Home is where our heart is. And the ability to create a heartfelt home wherever we are is in our hands.

In our final chapter, I'll share how I finally knew it was time to wrap up my Year by the Water and how I found a *Next* that was equally satisfying. You'll discover how you can keep your antenna up for what's next so you're always evolving, always creating a life you love.

28

Welcome What's *Next*

"I think I am quite ready for another adventure."

—BILBO BAGGINS

Guess what the third-most-frequently asked question on my Year by the Water was? *"When are you going to settle down?"*

My stock answer to that was, "Well, 'settle' means compromise and 'down' means depressed. Why would I do that?!"

I blew right by my year-end deadline. There were still places I hadn't been, people I hadn't met, experiences I hadn't had. For example, I still haven't house-boated on Lake Powell, Lake Havasu, and Lake Mead or visited the Hudson River Valley in fall to see the autumn leaves.

But then, something happened I didn't expect.

My sons and their wives called with good news . . . babies!

Tom and Patty asked if I'd come to Boulder and welcome Baby Natalia to the world.

Andrew and Miki asked if I'd come to Brooklyn to welcome Baby Hiro to the world.

Would I?! My new adventure had just shown up. I couldn't have predicted this turn of events and didn't plan it. But it was perfect in every way. Tolstoy wrote, "No matter what the work you are doing, be always ready to drop it. And plan it, so as to be able to leave it."

I had just spent eighteen months traveling where I wanted, when I wanted, experiencing and delighting in the discovery of new places and new people.

Now it was time for a satisfying full-circle experience with family. Instead of flying in for a week visit, it was time to *stay*. To weave myself into the fabric of family life. To be there to hold my new grandson through the night for the first month of his life. To see happy Natalia smile for the first time. To watch my son sit on the floor and play Legos with his son. To babysit so both couples could renew their romance and have fun date nights. To be there for Mateo's school Christmas party and see him singing "Rudolph the Red-Nosed Reindeer" with his buddies.

Aaahhh . . . the best of all worlds.

What's Your *Next* Adventure?

"The need for change bulldozed a road down the center of my brain."
— MAYA ANGELOU

Contrary to what Maya Angelou said, I think most changes don't bulldoze a path down the center of our brain, they appear as a crossroads and we often don't know which path to take.

It wasn't hard for me to say good-bye to my Year by the Water because my sons and their wives had just gifted me with a wonderfully congruent Next. Sometimes it's not so easy.

For example, a friend has been searching for her soul mate for years. She found him. He is everything she's wanted, and more. They are wonderfully in love, even though they had a few rough years taking care of family members with health challenges. Now, those trials are behind them. He is retiring after a thirty-year career as an airline captain. He's looking forward to traveling to warm places with my friend and treating her like a queen.

It's ideal . . . the only problem? She can't overcome her deeply embedded Puritan Work Ethic.

She told me, "Sam, after my divorce, I told myself I would never again rely on a man to 'take care of me.' I can't quite wrap my head around this." She built her business from scratch and put all three kids through college. After decades of nonstop biz dev, she can't stop saying yes to clients.

I said, "Look around. Your kids are grown and in a good place. You've had an incredibly rewarding and successful career. You are healthy and in love with a man who adores you. *Your dream has come true.* Yet, you're reverting to a 'scarcity' mindset instead of recognizing the abundance you've got and allowing yourself to enjoy it."

"I know, but . . ."

"Think ahead. How would you feel if something happened to you or to him and you didn't take advantage of this time together while you had the opportunity?"

She looked stricken. "I would regret it the rest of my life."

"Exactly. This is what Someday is all about. How we automatically postpone what would make us happy because we assume it will be there waiting for us later and we think we have 'more important' things to do now. But, there aren't more important things for you to do now. Is work more important than your time with him? Are clients? There is nothing preventing you from receiving and glorying in this love, except some old ways of thinking."

She got the point. And I'm happy to say, she just sent me a text saying, "Retirement is a glorious thing."

That was actually the first time I'd ever heard her use that word, and it gave me new insight into why she had initially resisted his generous offer to focus on her. She and I had joked that we would never retire. We're both speaker/authors/consultants. We've talked many times about how lucky we are to have a career we hope will last until the day we die.

I guess that's the point. She still *can* do this career. She's still in demand. Curtailing a booming business is not what she planned at this stage of her life. Plus, at some level, she may still feel retirement is something "old" people do, and she doesn't look or feel old.

However, life has given her a better offer. And one of the secrets to a successful life is to recognize a better offer when we get one and be open to receiving it and reveling in it . . . instead of sticking to a formerly prescribed plan.

May You Live a Graced Life

"You can't start the next chapter of your life
if you keep reading the old one."

—POSTER SEEN IN A LIBRARY

A key message of this book—and of the Life Hacks—is that a happy life is a mix of being present here and now—and at the same time—being open to what's next.

For example, I was on the phone with a fellow coach and mentioned how much I was loving my time in Maui. She asked, "Do you have plans to connect with Ram Dass while you're there?"

I laughed at the synchronicity of these dots connecting and said, "I didn't even know he was on island. I would love to meet Ram Dass. I just wrote about him in my book yesterday."

She said, "I'll see what I can do."

The next day, I get a message from her at ten fifteen in the morning, "Ram Dass is going to be at this beach at ten thirty. If you want to meet him, go now."

So I did. Which is how I had the unique pleasure of bobbing in the gentle Maui ocean with Ram Dass and about twelve other people.

You may know that Ram Dass had a stroke in 1997 when he was sixty-five years old. He said in an interview with the *San Francisco Gate*, "I did not care for my body. I cared for my psychology and my soul, but I never cared for my body. What I couldn't have anticipated was that stroke became the ending for a book I was working on: *Still Here: Embracing Aging, Changing, and Dying.*"

He admitted, "At first, I was depressed. There were three sufferings. The suffering of the body. The suffering of my ego, from being an independent person to being dependent. And spiritual suffering, because up until then, I had led a graced life ever since I met my guru in India. The stroke didn't look like grace. So I thought I was at the end of a graced life."

That day, as his friends gathered around him and carried him into the water, I saw a man living a graced life, despite the lingering physical effects of the stroke. He treaded water on his back in a buoyant life jacket and paddled around happily with his webbed aqua gloves. He threw his head back and sang up to the heavens, "Oh boy, oh boy, oh boy."

We chimed back, "Oh boy, oh boy, oh boy."

He smiled large and chanted, "Oh joy, oh joy, oh joy."

We sang back, "Oh joy, oh joy, oh joy."

Oh joy indeed. Grace indeed. What a privilege to meet this thought leader who has made such an enduringly positive difference for so many people around the world. Two of the insights Ram Dass is famous for is: "We are all just walking each other home" and "We are all affecting the world every moment, whether we mean to or not."

May we all walk (swim?) each other home and do our best to affect *our* world and *the* world a bit more positively on a daily basis.

May Your Next Be a Combination of Now and New

"If you don't step forward; you are always in the same place."

—Nora Roberts

I returned to Ram's favorite beach the following week. I wasn't about to pass up another opportunity to get in the ocean with him. I told him about my Year by the Water and how one of my most important lessons learned was that being happy isn't now *or* next; it's now *and* next.

He shook his head vehemently. "No . . . it's now." He gestured to the sand, as if to indicate *this* moment and said with force, "*Now. Now.*"

I heard what he was saying and I know he and many other spiritual teachers preach about the importance about living in the present moment. In fact, Osho said, "When you are here and now, not jumping ahead, the miracle has happened. To be in the moment is the miracle."

Yes, it is a miracle to put all our head chatter aside and be right here, right now.

And, as people in improv like to point out, I believe this is a "Yes, and." Being in the now *and occasionally being in the next* is also a miracle. I don't think it's one or the other. I think it's a sublime balance of both.

To my mind, having a meaningful past (something we are grateful for), a meaningful *now* (something we're experiencing, appreciating, and imprinting in the present moment), and a meaningful *next* (something we're looking forward to) is the best of *all* worlds. It's not one or the other. It's all three.

Eckhart Tolle talked about all the negative emotions—anxiety, stress, worry—caused by focusing too much on the future. But what if our future is bright? What if it is filled with positive things like anticipation, excitement, and eagerness?

He also talked about all the negative emotions—regret, guilt, grievances—caused by focusing too much on the past. But what if our past was a gift? What if it was filled with positive memories, people, and experiences?

I understand the importance of spending the *majority* of our time in the present. I also believe there is value in occasionally venturing to the "now and then" and the "now and in the future."

For example, reflecting on the places I visited, the people I met, and the blessed experiences I've had is a way to relive them all over again. As Queen Elizabeth said, "Good memories are our second chance at happiness." Who wouldn't want that?

And looking ahead at what could be next fills me with anticipation for the wonders that might wait around the next corner, over the next horizon.

I Was Blind and Now I See

"The only worse thing than being blind is having sight but no vision."
— HELEN KELLER

I've already set my next Next in motion. In a few weeks I'll be hosting a Someday Salon in Atlanta. The following day I'll be driving to Tuscumbia, Alabama. What's there?

This is where the teacher Anne Sullivan took her student Helen Keller, who had been blind since she was nineteen months old, to an old pump house by a lake. She started spelling the word "water" into Helen's hand in an effort to help her connect letters with objects' names.

At first, Helen thought her teacher was just playing a finger game. But as Sullivan kept tapping the letters into her hand, she had an epiphany that she eloquently described in her autobiography, "I stood still, my whole attention fixed upon the motions of her fingers. Suddenly I felt a misty consciousness—a thrill of returning thought—and somehow the mystery of language was revealed to me. I knew then that 'w-a-t-e-r' meant the cool something that was flowing over my hand. That living word awakened my soul, gave it light, hope, joy, set it free! There were barriers still, it is true, but barriers that could in time be swept away."

As a result of that breakthrough moment, the dots connected. Helen learned thirty words that first day and eventually learned to read, write, and speak. All that paved the way for her becoming an impassioned spokesperson for those with disabilities—and doing the work she was born to do.

I can't know this for sure, but I'm pretty sure my pilgrimage to Helen Keller's birthpace is going to turn into another "metaphor story."

Water was the breakthrough that helped Helen expand her world and make sense of her world.

My Year by the Water was a breakthrough that helped expand my world and helped me make sense of the world. It has led to me doing the work I was born to do.

I hope this book has been a breakthrough experience for you. I hope it has helped you connect dots that have expanded your world, and helped you make sense of your world.

I hope that puzzle pieces of happiness have fallen into place and you see your world with fresh eyes and a vision for how to be happier and live more fully . . . right here, right now.

During those years I was overscheduled, I was often blind to the world around me. I had mental and emotional blinders on. I was too focused on getting things done to see its everyday miracles. And if I wasn't seeing the miracles, I wasn't experiencing them or appreciating them fully.

It took a combination of a health scare, a downloaded dream with a start date, and uprooting my life to help me see the world with fresh eyes. What will it take for you?

Epilogue: Onward

"It is our choices that show us who we truly are,
far more than our abilities."

—J. K. ROWLING

We end as we began, with a story about a road trip. I was traveling from Colorado to California. My goal was to make it to Las Vegas the first night.

But that's not what happened.

It was sunny when I started out, so I was unprepared when a sudden snowstorm descended on mountainous Route 70. I turned on the windshield wipers and pulled the lever for the fluid to clear the road muck away. No fluid. Within seconds, the windshield was completely obscured. I couldn't see a thing. I desperately rolled the window down, stuck my head out, and tried to navigate the winding highway. Semi-trucks barreled by, blaring their horns at me. I knew I should pull over, but I didn't dare stop as I had no idea what was on the side of the road, parked cars, a guardrail, snowbanks, nothing?

Thankfully, a good Samaritan pulled alongside, opened his window, and yelled, "What's happening?!"

"I can't see! I can't see!"

"There's an exit up ahead," he shouted. "I'll get in front of you and flash my brake lights. Follow me."

I could barely see his flashing red lights, but was able to follow him to the exit, where we both pulled over. I got out of the car, shaking. He cleared off my windshield, guided me to the closest gas station, and filled my windshield-wiper fluid. I gave him a big tip even though he graciously said it wasn't necessary. I told him, "You probably just saved my life. It's the least I can do."

I sat there, sending up thanks for that good Samaritan, relieved and grateful to have survived that scary close call. I needed to get back on the road though if I was going to make it to Las Vegas that night. Hours later, I was driving through a mountain pass in Utah. It was dark, the road was icy, and I was emotionally exhausted, but I still had a couple hundred miles to drive.

Then, just like that first day of my Year by the Water, a thought bubble appeared above my head. "Why drive on an icy road in the dark when you're tired?"

This time, I didn't think twice about changing my mind and backing out of a commitment. Let's see. What's more important? My health. My life. Or losing some money on a hotel room I wasn't going to get a refund for? No-brainer decision.

As soon as I listened to my gut and honored my instincts, SerenDestiny showed up.

I found a room in a quaint hotel ten minutes away. I woke up rested the next morning and walked next door to get breakfast at a 5.0 Yelp-rated family restaurant. As I was writing in my journal, the waitress stopped by to refill my cup of coffee, "Are you going to Zion?"

"*Zion?!*"

"You know it's only an hour away?"

I hadn't known, but thankfully I now had room for whims and could answer the call. Which is how I found myself driving into the most stunning national park I'd ever seen. If you've been to Zion, you know it's gasp-out-loud gorgeous. It was an uncommonly warm winter day and off-season, which meant I got to experience the park in her full beauty with no crowds.

As I learned to do on my Year by the Water, I asked locals for "What do you suggest?" advice. One told me there was a vacancy at a one-of-a-kind hotel that was normally sold out, so I impulsively decided to stay an extra day.

A park ranger told me, "If you do one thing today, hike up to Emerald Pools. The trail leads to a natural waterfall/spring . . . a real anomaly in a desert." Which is how I found myself hiking up a twisting trail along a streambed, where everything I saw was for the first time, literally and figuratively. I came to my senses and reveled in nature's wonderland.

As I gazed up at the water pouring over the cliff face, I remembered that Zion was #1 on my dad's bucket list, one of the national parks he never got to see. As I gloried in this unplanned gift of an experience, I sent up a silent prayer, "*This one's for you, Dad. This one's for you.*"

Continue to Apply the Ten Life Hacks to Change Your Life—for Good

"The most courageous act is still to think for yourself."
—Coco Chanel

It wasn't until the next day, as I drove out of the mountain valley, that it hit me. *This* was the bookend to my Year by the Water. I was ending it as I began it. I had subconsciously done every one of the Life Hacks on that trip and turned a Someday into a Today.

EVALUATE: I evaluated the situation and decided that driving on an icy road at night when I was tired was hurting my health and happiness and made a change—for good.

GENERATE: I generated a meaningful alternative to what was putting me at risk. Finding a hotel where I could be safe became my top True Priority and my top Time Priority.

ABDICATE: I abdicated my plan to drive all the way to Las Vegas. I stopped watering the dead plant of regret that I wasn't going to get a refund for my prepaid hotel in Vegas.

INITIATE: I initiated a new plan of action and trusted I could figure things out. I didn't know where I would stay when I decided to stop driving, I just knew it wasn't going to be Las Vegas!

CELEBRATE: I absolutely celebrated being safe and sound in a warm, comfy bed instead of being out on that highway, driving on ice. And I received and reveled in the grandeur of Zion.

AFFILIATE: I gratefully *accepted* the help of that good Samaritan and *asked* for help in Zion by seeking advice. And I created a community of one on that solo hike to Emerald Pools, which resulted in a memorable connection with that majestic place and meaningful experience.

INTEGRATE: Zion was a "best of both worlds" blended work and recreation experience. I combined my passion (nature and outdoor adventure) with my profession (writing).

INNOVATE: Proceeding with an open mind (instead of the end in mind) created a rewarding experience that was better than anything I could have planned.

NEGOTIATE: My original hotel room in Zion looked out at the parking lot. I called the front desk and kindly asked if they might have a room with a view, as I was hoping to wake up and "write to the mountains." The friendly clerk upgraded me for no extra charge to a suite overlooking a mountain range lit by the full moon. Never would have happened if I hadn't asked.

RELOCATE: I "jumped ship" and relocated to a better town, better hotel room, and better overall experience instead of staying stuck with a situation that was was creating dissonance.

Happiness is Not a One-and-Done Process

"The way we do anything is the way we do everything."

—MARTHA BECK

I hope this book has inspired you to do more of what's important to you so you're creating the quality of life you want, need, and deserve.

Keep this book handy, on your desk or nightstand. If for some reason you're feeling blue or unsure what to do, open it to a page—any page. Chances are, you'll discover a quote or story with just the right words to lift your spirits.

How about one more story to center you in your resolve to do what matters—now, not later?

I was speaking in Boston when a woman asked if there was any place I missed on my Year by the Water? "Yes, I always wanted to visit Walden Pond and somehow never made it there."

She said, "You know it's an hour away?"

Well, blow me over with a feather. I hadn't known. I jumped online, changed my reservation, and rented a car to drive to Concord, Massachusetts. I couldn't miss this opportunity (it was only an hour away!) to walk where Thoreau walked and write where he wrote. Little did I know I was going to swim where he swam.

The drive there was rainy and blustery. The little voice inside (who always has our best interests at heart) whispered, "Forget today. Get up early tomorrow and go then."

So, that's what I did. My intuition proved right, yet again. The morning dawned bright and sunny. I got to the park as soon as it opened. There were only three other cars in the entire lot.

As I grabbed my backpack and locked my car, a man walked by in his swim trunks, with a towel slung over his shoulder. This was October in New England. A man in a swimsuit was about the last thing I expected to see. Incredulous, I asked, "Is the water warm enough to swim?"

"It is if you go to the end of the lake by the cove where Thoreau's cabin is. It's shallower there and a bit warmer."

I set out in that direction, striding along the pine-needle-covered path under a canopy of trees. I rounded a bend and there was the calm, crystal clear cove. The fall colors were perfectly reflected in the mirror-like surface of the lake.

I hadn't brought a swimsuit with me, but it was such a perfect day, I thought, "Who knows if or when I'll ever be back?" So, I *went in.*

I will always be glad I did. I will remember for the rest of my days floating on my back and gazing up at the blue sky and puffy white clouds, filled with the spirit of Thoreau's muse.

Clothes dry. Memories don't.

Get Off the Shore of Life. Go In.

"Four of the worst words you can say are, 'If I had only . . .'"

—JEFF BEZOS

Folks, we're not here to stand on the shore. We're here to get up, get out, and go in.

I hope these stories have inspired you to stop waiting and start creating a life more in alignment with what matters to you.

I hope these insights have given you the clarity and courage to make small changes right where you are, right now, to create a more fulfilling life.

I hope these Life Hacks help you prevent regrets that would haunt you in the end.

When tennis champion Serena Williams was in the middle of a run at a historic Grand Slam, she discovered she was pregnant. This wasn't part of her plan; however, she decided to revel in the good news and partner with what was happening. She told reporters, "My story isn't over yet."

Neither is yours. You can revise your story and create a new story anytime you want. The key is to do it one day at a time.

When all is said and done, when you're looking back on your life, one thing is clear.

You will never regret putting yourself in your own story and doing more of what makes you happier, healthier, and more fulfilled; you'll only regret not doing it . . . sooner.

You've got this. Onward.

Acknowledgments

"When you drink the water, remember the well."
—CHINESE PROVERB

Anyone who has written a book understands why authors often thank a long list of friends, family, and business associates who sustain us during the roller-coaster years it can take to produce a book. When our project is finally finished, we want to make sure they know how much they're appreciated. So, heartfelt thanks to the following individuals for being a wellspring of strength, smarts, and support.

Cheri Grimm, my sister and business manager, for continuing to be there for me in more ways than I can possibly express. It's a fun and rewarding ride, isn't it, sis?

Agent Laurie Liss, for her continuing vision and advocacy of my literary career and books.

Daniela Rapp, Jennifer Enderlin, Joe Rinaldi, and the St. Martin's Press team for believing in me and this project and helping it get out into the world.

My sons Tom and Andrew, their delightful and talented wives Patty and Miki, and their happy, healthy kids who have the light on in their eyes—and who put the light on in mine.

My longtime friends who create a "rising tide raising all involved" life that just keeps getting better and better: Judy Gray, Mary LoVerde, Denise Brosseau, Dianne Gerard, Jeanne Sullivan, Joan Fallon, Mariah Burton Nelson, Sue Liebenow, Lee Self, Lori Bachman, Peggy Cappy. Thank you for keeping me smiling, for reminding me to practice what I teach, for shared memories and adventures, and for gifting me with what really matters, enduring friendships.

And mahalo to the people I interviewed along the way for allowing me to share your stories. May your insights motivate others to lead the life of their dreams now, not someday.

Resources

SOMEDAY Made Me Do It: What's Your Story?

"If you are given only one opportunity to speak,
be certain your voice is heard."

—ELIZABETH GILBERT

While browsing in Stinson Beach Books, the owner asked if I was looking for anything in particular. I asked "Any books about fulfilling dreams?" and told her about my journey.

With a big smile on her face, she walked me over to a special section with Staff Picks, picked up a book and handed it to me. It was Elizabeth Gilbert's *Eat, Pray, Love Made Me Do It.*

As the jacket copy said, "Since its electrifying debut, Elizabeth Gilbert's *Eat Pray Love* has empowered millions of readers to set out on paths they never thought possible, in search of their own best selves. Here, nearly fifty of those readers share their transformative, deeply inspiring stories of how they stepped out of their old lives to fulfill long-held dreams."

My dream is that my next book is *SOMEDAY Made Me Do It* filled with *your* stories. Stories of what you decided to start, stop, or do differently. Stories of how you acted on your dreams and True Priorities and made your life more of what you wanted it to be.

That's a big dream, but that's what this book is about, right?

Please take a few minutes to let me know how this book has impacted you. Who knows? Your story may be just what someone needs to hear to put themselves in their own story.

Make your voice heard by sending your insights to Sam@IntrigueAgency.com. With your permission, we might share it with others so they're inspired to do more of what puts the light on in their eyes, starting Today, not Someday.

READERS' GUIDE FOR *SOMEDAY IS NOT A DAY IN THE WEEK*

"Progress is a nice word. But change is its motivator."

— ROBERT KENNEDY

The best way to make progress is to ask probing questions that prompt us to change—for good.

And the best way to do that is with an accountability buddy or support group.

You may want to buy this book with a friend, a book club, or for employees in your company.

Agree to read a chapter a week and then discuss it over a meal, at a staff meeting, or on a walk-talk.

These questions can facilitate a far-ranging conversation that leads to valuable aha's for all involved.

If you'd like our free Faciliatator's Guide on how to host a Someday Salon or Someday Book Club, contact us at Cheri@IntrigueAgency .com. We'll be happy to send it to you.

Life Hack 1. EVALUATE Your Happiness History

1. **Play Hooky for a Day**
   1. How would you spend your free day or afternoon? What would you do if the people you're responsible for would be taken care of, and there would be *no* repercussions?
   2. What are three things you would *not* do on your day of hooky? Why?
   3. What were your answers to the boxes in the Happiness Quiz? Were they surprises?

2. **Remember the Golden Days**
   1. What were your top five priorities? What do you spend the most time on? Do your lists match? If so, how so? How are you able to live in alignment with what matters to you?
   2. If your lists don't match, why? What's going on to cause the disparity?
   3. What questions from the Happiness Interview produced an aha? What insights did you get from delving into what is contributing to, or compromising, your happiness?

3. **Adopt a Sense of Urgency**
   1. Which of the reasons people gave for *waiting* resonated with you? Please elaborate how each particular reason has prevented you from doing what would make you happier?
   2. Did you do the pretend S.E.E.? What would you do if you only had a week to live? Is there some way you can actually do that, even part of it, now not someday? How so?
   3. When is a time you didn't wait to do what was important to you? What gave you the clarity and confidence to act instead of to procrastinate? How did it make you feel?
   4. Who do you know who you think of as "happy"? Who is a shining example of someone who DOES what they want now, not someday? What can you learn from their example?

Life Hack 2. GENERATE a Today, Not Someday Dream

4. **Clarify What You Want**
    1. Were you fortunate enough to have a calling, mission, or passion project downloaded to you? What was it? Did you act on it? Why or why not? How has that affected your life?
    2. What is the mission statement you crafted? Where will you keep it "in sight, in mind" so it can help you make decisions that are in alignment with your purpose and True Priorities?
    3. What do you want more of in your life? What would make your life more fulfilling? How will you give time to it to this week— instead of floating and waiting to do it someday?

5. **Put a Date on the Calendar**
    1. What would you like to experience or achieve by the end of this year? What is your Today, Not Someday dream? When will you launch it? What "do-date" did you put on your calendar?
    2. Now, start filling in the W's . . . where, when, who, what, why. Who will you discuss this with so they can help you fill in the blanks so your dream goes from vague to vividly clear?
    3. Where will you post your dream so it stays "in sight, in mind," and you are constantly re-inspired to do what you said you wanted to do?

Life Hack 3. ABDICATE Outdated Beliefs and Behaviors

6. **Just Say No to Naysayers**
    1. Do you have a naysayer who is telling you it's wrong, foolish, or selfish to pursue your dream? Who is that person? What are they saying? What's their real agenda? How has this person impacted you, up until now? Have they caused you to question yourself? Have they undermined your clarity, your courage, to grow and move forward?
    2. What will you do to speak up for yourself the next time this

person tries to undermine you? Or, what will you do to disassociate from this person or reduce their power over you?

3. Who is a cheerleader who supports what you're doing? How does this person help you grow and encourage you to be all you can be? How will you spend more time with this person so they give you the energy, tools, clarity, and confidence to proceed?

7. **Let It Go, Let It Go, Let It Go**

1. How do you feel when you walk into your home? Where would your home rate on the Clutter (1) to Clean (10) Scale? How does that affect you? Do you feel guilty, stressed, or frustrated with how things have piled up? Or do you feel proud, at peace with how well-designed, organized, and beautiful your space is?

2. How much time do you spend cleaning, repairing, buying, renovating your stuff? Is that a source of enjoyment, a burden and chore, or something in between? Explain.

3. Are you ready to downsize your home and/or release some belongings? How will you do that? Who else does this have an impact on? How will you negotiate this with them? What could you do with the resources that would be freed up when you have less to take care of?

8. **Stop Driving into Hurricanes**

1. Can you relate to the "Why am I driving into a hurricane" story? What commitments are you keeping because you said you would? What are the consequences of that?

2. Is there a time you "broke a promise" and, instead of it being a catastrophe, it actually led to a better situation? Please describe what happened.

3. What is a stormy situation you're in right now? Do you keep driving into this hurricane because you want to honor your commitment? Can you approach those you've committed to, tell the truth as fast as you can, and explore options that have the potential to be a win for all involved?

Life Hack 4. INITIATE Daily Actions that Move Your Life Forward

9. You Don't Have to Know to Go

1. Do you see yourself as brave? Why or why not? When is a time you tried something new and it worked out well? How can you tap back into that confidence and tell yourself, "If I did it before, I can do it again?"

2. Were you brought up to see the world as a scary, dangerous place or a safe, adventurous place? How has that impacted your willingness to venture out on your own?

3. What is something new you want to try? Are you getting conflicting advice? What's your gut telling you? What if you took the bolder of the options and figured it out on the way?

10. Honor the Nudges, Connect the Dots

1. Do you make room for whims? Why or why not? When was a time you honored a nudge and acted on your intuition? What happened as a result?

2. Do you think this is a lot of hooey? Does your intellect override your instincts? Or, do you agree that if we have a sixth sense that alerts us to what's wrong, we also have a sixth sense that alerts us to what's right? What are your beliefs about this?

3. How will you honor the instincts that have your best interests at heart? How will you connect the dots, act on "coincidences" that beat the odds, and align with congruent individuals and opportunities that "feel right"?

11. Put Yourself in Your Own Story

1. Would you say you're putting yourself in your own story? How so?

2. When or how do you take yourself out of the story? Why?

3. What was modeled for you about serving others? How has that supported or sabotaged your happiness? How will you strike a healthier balance between serving others and yourself? What is something you'll do "just for yourself" this week?

12. Beware of the Rubber Band of Routine Snapping Back

1. Have you found that, despite your best intentions, the Rubber Band of Routine has snapped back and you've reverted to old ways? How so?

2. How will you use language to focus on what you *do* want instead of what you *don't* want? For example, how could you turn *empty* days into *open* days?

3. What metrics will you assign to your dream so you have a measurable way to hold yourself accountable? How will you give yourself a "second chance" to get this change right and persevere to bring your life into alignment with your True Priorities and avoid reverting to old habits?

Life Hack 5. CELEBRATE What's Right with Life, Right Here, Right Now

13. Live in Day-Right Compartments

1. Do you have a morning practice? If so, what is it? If not, why not?

2. Do you find yourself getting caught up in the busyness of the world? Do you feel you're losing connection with yourself and others? How so?

3. What will you do to create a mindful ritual in the morning to get your day off to a good start? Will you belly-breathe or bring your mind to the present moment by using a Someday Journal (or the equivalent) to keep the Happiness Hacks top of mind?

14. Get Out of Your Head and Come to Your Senses

1. When was the last time you saw something as if for the first or last time? Describe what happened and what it felt like.

2. Do you have a busy, stressful life? What is the ongoing impact of rushing, rushing, rushing—and always feeling "an hour late and a dollar short"?

3. Would you say you have "juice" in your camera? Do you look at the world with fresh eyes? When, where, and how will you get out of your head and come to your senses?

15. **Get a Move On**
    1. Would you say you appreciate your freedom of movement or do you take it for granted? What are you currently doing to take care of your body and health? Elaborate.
    2. What are you doing that is harming your body or jeopardizing your freedom of movement? Sitting? Smoking? Eating and drinking the wrong things? What?
    3. Do you have a car? Is it a source of frustration or a source of freedom? When and where will you go for fun—walking, driving, biking, flying, or training—*because you can?*

16. **Free Up Time for Fun**
    1. What do you do for fun? Do you have a hobby? Sing? Garden? What? How often do you do this? How does it contribute to the quality of your life?
    2. What did you *used to do* for recreation? Is that out of your life now? Why? Do you feel it's frivolous, that you have more important things to do? Explain.
    3. How will you carve out time to have a good time? How will you bring more joy into your life? When, where, and how will you do something that puts the light on in your eyes?

17. **Be Wealthy in What Matters**
    1. Growing up, what were the messages you received about money?
    2. On a scale of 1 to 10, how satisfied are you with the amount of money you make and have? Do you have "enough" or is lack of money undermining your quality of life? Explain. What is your "number"? What do you envision happening when you reach it?
    3. How are you wealthy in what matters, right here, right now? Give an example of what you will do to imprint and appreciate your "good fortune" this week. Has a dream come true and you haven't really acknowledged it? How will you rectify that?

Life Hack 6. AFFILIATE with People Who Have Your Back and Front

18. Launch Your Ship in Public

1. So, what is that venture you want to launch? Who has supported you, cheered you on? What have they done to help you achieve your goal and do what's important to you?

2. Who has cautioned you, told you ("for your own good") that what you want to do won't work or isn't a good idea? What impact has that had on you?

3. How will you take your dream public and give others a chance to jump on your bandwagon? Will you create a vision board and/or host a Today, Not Someday party? Where did you post your vision so it stays "in sight, in mind"?

19. Create a Community of One

1. When was a time you had a room—or road—of your own? What did it mean to you? Where do you go *now* to escape? What do you do there? Why is it important to you?

2. Are you an introvert, extrovert, or ambivert? How do you take responsibility for getting the right mix of being social and being solitary?

3. Can you be alone without being lonely? Are you comfortable going places by yourself because you can connect with your surroundings and turn strangers into friends? How so?

Life Hack 7. INTEGRATE Your Passion and Profession

20. Blend Your Work and Recreation

1. Did you used to see your work and recreation as separate? If so, why so? If not, how did you get clear you could have the best of both worlds by combining them?

2. What skills, talents, hobbies do you have that you can integrate into your work? How can you integrate your passion and purpose into your profession so it benefits all involved?

3. What do you currently work hard at? How, like the realtor/tennis player, can you combine your job and joy and make it more rewarding now, not later?

21. Don't Wait for Work You Love; Create Work You Love

1. Do you love your job? Do you feel you're adding value and contributing? How so?

2. If you don't find your work satisfying, why not? What talents or skills are you not having an opportunity to use or get credit for?

3. What are your Four I's? How could you leverage them into a paying career where you get paid to do what you're good at? What is your next step? Will you visit crafts fairs to see how other people have turned a passion into a profession? Elaborate.

Life Hack 8. NEGOTIATE for What You Want, Need, and Deserve

22. Stop Trying to Make People Happy; You're Not Chocolate

1. Are you too nice for your own good? Are you a people-pleaser who orders pasta you don't want? How so? How does this impact you and the people around you?

2. Have you been taking yourself out of the picture—and habitually putting others first? Was that modeled for you growing up? Why do you do that? What are the consequences?

3. What is a specific situation where you haven't been clear about what you want? How will you rectify that by saying what *you* want up front, now and in the future?

23. If You Don't Ask, the Answer's Always No

1. When is a time you asked for something you wanted—whether it was a promotion, project lead, or pay raise? How did you prepare? What was the result?

2. When is a time you waited for someone to "do the right thing," act on your behalf, or give you what you deserved? As Dr. Phil would say, "How'd that work for you?"

3. What is a situation you're unhappy with right now? Which of the Four A's have you used? How will you alter the situation by using the Five P's of Persuasion to increase the likelihood of improving this situation?

Life Hack 9. INNOVATE a Fresh Start

24. Quit Watering Dead Plants

1. Is the majority of your life out of your control and not to your liking? How so? Does this challenging time have a timeline? Can you "make your mind a deal it can't refuse" so you are able to keep things in perspective?

2. What do you currently do to maintain a positive perspective, to have something to look forward to in bleak times? How do you stay focused on what you *can* control?

3. Are there dead plants you can stop watering? What can you quit what is compromising your quality of life? How can you innovate a fresh start if you are going through dark times to keep the light on in your eyes?

25. Do the Opposite of Your Always

1. Would you describe your life, career, or long-term relationships as an aircraft carrier? How so? Is it a successful carrier? Are people counting on you to stay on the carrier?

2. Are you ready to fly off your carrier now and then so you can be by yourself or so you can be yourself? Where on earth would you like to go? What do you want to do?

3. What is a local place that could be your Utah, the Third Place where you could go to work on a priority project? When will you go there? What will you work on there?

Life Hack 10. RELOCATE to Greener Pastures

26. Give Yourself a GFS—Geographic Fresh Start

1. Would you say you're a roots person or a wings person? What does that mean to you?

2. Are you happy where you are in your current home? In your neighborhood, city, and state? If so, what do you like about it? If not, what don't you like about it?

3. If you could move, where would you go? What would it take for you to move? Imagine it in full detail. Write out the steps to move this from being a vague idea to a vivid reality.

27. Come Full Circle

1. When was the last time you were in your hometown? What memories did it bring back? Did you reconnect with people that influenced you? Did it catalyze a new creative direction that could be a satisfying full-circle way to come home to who you truly are?

2. What used to light you up but now feels like it might be a retreat or regression to "go back there"? Do you worry it's thinking small instead of thinking big? Could it actually be you're going "home" to who you are at your core, your best self?

3. Do you agree with Ram Dass that we can be "at home" wherever we are and that "home" is a mindset, not a location? Where do you feel most at home?

28. Welcome What's *Next*

1. Are you ready for a fresh start, a new adventure? What might that be?

2. Do you agree with philosophers that living in the now is the miracle—or do you believe happiness can be a balance of the *now* and the *next*?

3. How will you keep your antenna up for a *Next* that's in alignment with your True Priorities? What will you say to yourself when that opportunity arises so you act on it?

About the Author

+ Sam Horn, Founder/CEO of the Intrigue Agency, is on a mission to help people create a quality life-work that adds value for all involved.

+ Her impressive client lists includes National Geographic, NASA, Capital One, Intel, Nationwide, Boeing, Four Seasons Resorts, Cisco, and National Governors Association.

+ Her books—*Tongue Fu!*®, *POP!*, and *Washington Post* bestseller *Got Your Attention?*—have been featured in *The New York Times*, *Forbes*, *Fast Company*, and on NPR and endorsed by Dan Pink, Stephen Covey, Tony Robbins, and Marshall Goldsmith.

+ As former Executive Director of the world-renowned Maui Writers Conference, and Pitch Coach for Springboard Enterprises (which has helped entrepreneurs receive $8.8 billion in funding), she has helped hundreds of clients create quality books and high-stakes presentations for TED-MED, TEDx, SXSW, Wisdom 2.0, Google, and Facebook.

+ Sam hosts Someday Salons across the country for organizations who would like to facilitate meaningful conversations about what really matters. To arrange for Sam to share her inspiring keynote with your organization, contact Cheri@IntrigueAgency.com

+ Would you like to attend a Someday Weekend to do a deep dive into identifying a meaningful *Next* that could make money and a difference? Visit www.SerenDestiny.com

+ Sam continues to be a season-bird, following the sun, and living by the water in Hawaii, Colorado, California, and New York. To receive Sam's newsletter, stay updated on her travels, and to find out when she'll be in your area, visit www.SamHorn.com.